Applied Java Programming

Applied Java Programming

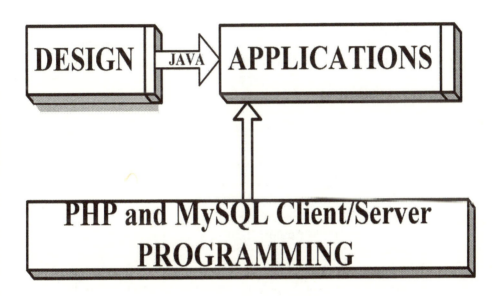

DESIGN →JAVA→ APPLICATIONS

PHP and MySQL Client/Server
PROGRAMMING

Edward Hill, Jr.

iUniverse, Inc.
New York Lincoln Shanghai

Applied Java Programming

iUniverse books may be ordered through booksellers or by contacting:

iUniverse
2021 Pine Lake Road, Suite 100
Lincoln, NE 68512
www.iuniverse.com
1-800-Authors (1-800-288-4677)

ISBN: 978-0-595-45028-2 (pbk)
ISBN: 978-0-595-89342-3 (ebk)

Printed in the United States of America

Contents

Preface

Use as a Textbook

The design and analysis of efficient programs has been recognized as a key subject in computing. The study of programming machines is part of the core curriculum in computer science and computer engineering. Typically, in programs using Java as the base language Java computer programming is introduced early in computer science curriculums. In this case the Java course covers a strong introduction and emphasizes many of the advance features in the language. At the end of the Java programming language course students are expected to program applications using the language. Programming applications in a programming language requires the use of data structures. This text book introduces the students to minimal data structures for use in the design and implementation of applied application programs. This "Applied Java Programming" text book is designed to integrate learning to program Java [10] with applied programming. Selected data structures topics [9] are use to facilitate a beginner applied programming in Java. All exercises are programming problems. Programming problems are used as exercises to enforce a programming paradigm. A high percent of learning to program is highly correlated with the practice of designing and implementing programs using appropriate data structures for specific requirements. The translator or compiler will enhance the student knowledge through the trail and error process of removing errors from their programs. Emphasis is on defining Java constructs with the appropriate data structures and their use in programming applied applications. Students are encouraged to program all the exercises at the end of each Chapter. Also students are encouraged to program their own applications to enhance their knowledge base. The idea is to program as many applications as possible using various Java constructs with data structures to improve programming skills in the Java programming language and the art of designing and implementing applied applications. Emphasis is placed on programming client/server web applications.

Many enterprises involve an environment with computer networks that store large amounts of data in relational databases. Performance is a key issue in operating an enterprise that requires fast processing of business transactions. Cost is another enterprise issue. The perspective of this text book is to present tools with reasonable performance attributes at minimum cost to develop applications. This textbook focuses on open source or fee software. A simple network is configured using the Apache server to manage the client/server environment. Most enterprises with large amounts of data require a relational database to store data. A relational database MySQL server is introduced to store and retrieve client/server applications data. MySQL is introduces because applications developed using its Structured Query Language (SQL) database engine is portable to many computer platforms at minimal cost. A script language called Hypertext Processor (PHP) is introduced to develop web applications. The script language PHP is introduced because many of the constructs are the same or very close to the Java programming language. The second major reason for the use of PHP is portability for many plat forms running Microsoft Windows, Linux, UNIX, and Mac Operating Systems.

The core Chapters in this textbook are Chapter 3 on **Selected Java Utilities Package and Bit Manipulation**, Chapter 4 on **Selected Collections**, and Chapter 5 on **Implementing an e-Business Application**. Chapter 3 is integrated with 5 programs to emphasize major methods in the Java Utilities Package. Chapter 4 integrates two programs that use Collections. Chapter 3 and Chapter 4 are supported by an Appendix tutorial called **class Vector**. Chapter 5 on **Implementing an e-Business Application** defines and implements a client/server business application. Chapter 5 is supported by Appendices tutorials called **Selected Hypertext Mark-up Language (HTML) Tutorial**, **Selected PHP Tutorial**, **Selected MySQL Tutorial**, and a **Selected Network Tutorial**.

World Wide Web Access

All of the code for Applied Java Programming is on the Internet at Virtual Hill Analysis Computer Consultant Web site http://www.vhacc.com. Please download all the code then run each program as you read the text. Make changes to the code examples and see what happens. Interact with the Java compiler to resolve various kinds of errors. Analyze the changes to the code. This parametric approach to programming is a great heuristic to learning by doing programming.

Selected Subject Content

An analysis has been performed on many topics in the area of teaching students to program using the Java programming language. Selected subject content is used to minimize the time required to develop Java programming skills. The idea is to develop a strong Java programming basis. Given a strong Java programming basis other subject content can be added as extended knowledge as a part of the heuristics of programming applied Java applications. In this text book selected subject content is used to enforce this learning paradigm.

Prerequisites

This book is written assuming that the reader comes to it with certain knowledge. It is assumed that the reader is familiar with algebra. The reader understands that the text is designed for students willing to program Java, use simple data structures, program HTML, program minimal PHP script language, program minimal MySQL including:

- Variables and expressions
- Methods
- Decision structures (such as if-statements, and switch-statements)
- Iteration structures (for-loops and while-loops)
- File input and output
- Class definition and use
- Object definition and use
- Package definition and use
- Event definition and use
- Graphic User Interface definition and use
- Thread definition and use
- Network configuration
- Script language programming
- Client-server programming.

For the Instructor

This book is intended primarily as a textbook for an applied Java Programming course in which the students have object programming language skills.

1. Applied Java Programming

1.1. Presentation Model

This textbook assumes the reader has basic Java knowledge to write constructs, build Java elements, control structures, methods, object-oriented programs, arrays and string, class inheritance, graphics programs, with exception handling, with multithreading, and file input and output. [10] The Java programming language is used to develop fast proto-types for e-business applications. These e-business applications operate on servers. The Java programmer uses variants of Java constructs to write PHP programs that connect to relational databases in a client server context.

1.2. Selected Data Structures

Linked stacks, queues, and deques are included for use in explaining many of the concepts in the presentation model. These structures are used to illustrate many of the classes in the java.util package.

1.3. Selected Bit Manipulations

A bit, or binary digit, is the smallest unit of information processed by a computer and consists of a single 0 or 1. A byte consists of a set of adjacent bits. The capacity of computer memory and storage devices is usually expressed in bytes. Bit manipulations operations are defined on a set of bits.

1.4. Use of Collections

Programmers create and manipulate data structures. Each element of each data structure is created dynamically with new. The data structures are modified by directly manipulating their elements and references to their elements. Java collections give the programmer access to packaged data structures as well as algorithms for manipulating those data structures.

1.5. Selected PHP and HTML

Selected Hypertext Processor (PHP) and Hypertext Markup Language (HTML) are integrated and used as a basis for developing and implementing e-business applications. The PHP script language constructs are close to the Java programming language constructs. These similarities are used to fast prototype e-business applications. The e-business applications are designed to be executed by-way of a web browser. Use of web browsers for access allows the applications to be placed on servers. Use of PHP, HTML, and Java supports many computer platforms at no cost for the software that implements the applications.

1.5.1. What is PHP?

Many of the constructs in PHP are borrowed from other languages such as The C programming language, shell, Perl, and the Java programming language. It is a hybrid language, taking the best features from other languages to create a powerful scripting language. PHP applications may be implemented by embedding it in HTML. [13]

1.5.1.1. HTML Embedding

Selected HTML is detailed to explain how PHP is embedded in the language. A basic HTML code consists of tags that direct the browser parser of the text. HTML tags are defined by opening the tag with the tag name enclosed in angle brackets. Tags are closed with the tag name enclosed in an open angle bracket, followed by a forward slash, followed by the tag name, and closed with a close angle bracket. A HTML document is opened with a tag <HTML>. HTML documents are closed with a tag </HTML>. The head of the HTML document is designated with a <HEAD> tag. The main body of an HTML document is opened with a <BODY> tag. Each tag has a set of controls that are coded in the tag angle bracket to define the context of the tag. Information on HTML is detailed in [13]. A HTML Tutorial in Appendix D details selected information.

1.5.2. How to Write a Web Application With PHP?

Web applications are implemented with PHP by embedding the PHP code in a HTML document. A PHP tag <?php is used to open a PHP programming segment. A PHP tag ?> is used to close a PHP programming segment. The HTML browser executes the HTML tags. When a PHP open tag is recognized the browser invokes the PHP translator to execute the PHP code until a PHP close tag is recognized.

After the PHP close tag is recognized the browser switches to the browser interpreter to execute the browser tags that maybe generated by the PHP code segment. [11]

1.5.3. Databases with PHP

A PHP construct is used to connect to databases. After the database is connected other PHP constructs are used to access the databases. In web applications the PHP code must be enclosed in the PHP open and close tag for the browser to interpret the document. [11] A PHP Tutorial in Appendix E details selected information.

1.6. Selected MySQL

Selected MySQL is integrated with PHP, HTML, and Java as a basis for developing and implementing e-business applications. MySQL is an open source relational database management system (RDBMS). This RDBMS maybe connected to the PHP script language. This RDBMS is used to fast prototype e-business applications. The e-business applications are designed to be executed by-way-of a web browser. Use of web browsers for access allows the applications to be placed on servers. Use of MySQL, PHP, HTML, and Java supports many computer platforms at no cost for the software that implements the applications. [11, 12, 13]

1.6.1. What is MySQL?

MySQL is an open source relational database management system. The goal of MySQL is to make superior data management software available and affordable for all. MySQL operates in a client or networked environment using a client/server architecture. Therefore, it is compatible for e-business applications. [12] A MySQL Tutorial in Appendix F details selected information.

1.6.2. Database Connectivity

There are many ways to connect to a RDBMS. MySQL is chosen hear because it is an open source RDBMS that can be connected with PHP. Connection through PHP allows us to access it from a server by the way of a browser. The open source is congruent with our aim of minimizing web application cost. [11, 12]

1.6.3. Selected SQL

A selected subset of Structured Query Language (SQL) commands is detailed to implement an e-business application. SQL is used to access the RDBMS connected in PHP. The MySQL database engine parses the SQL commands and returns the requested information to PHP that transmits it to the HTML browser. [11, 12]

1.7. Selected Server Software

Apache-Tomcat is detailed to explain the role of server software in e-business applications. Emphasis is placed on Apache-Tomcat because it is free and portable on most platforms operating under the Microsoft Windows, Linux, or UNIX operating system. A Network Tutorial in Appendix G details selected information.

1.8. e-Business Application

The term e-business application is any client/server application that is accessed through a web browser. The application allows users access that includes the storage and retrieval of data from a relational database management system.

1.8.1. Implement a Client/Server Application

A simple client/server application is implemented to illustrate many of the ideas detailed in this textbook. The code for the application is detailed in Chapter 5 and Appendix H. The application is implemented on a server machine running the Linux Fedora operating system with the PHP script language and the MySQL relational database management system. This e-business application can be ported to any server running the PHP script language translator and the MySQL relational database management system.

2. Selected Data Structures: Stacks, Queues and Deques

The stack, queue, and deque linear structures are allocated using the sequential-allocation method of storage. These structures are accessed with sequential methods. Sequential data structures are reviewed to increase understanding of linked data structures. In Chapter 4 we detail linked-allocation and linked access methods for vectors, stacks, and queues using the Java List Class.

2.1. Stacks

One of the most important linear structures of variable size is the stack. In this structure, we are allowed to delete an element from and add an element to occur only at one end. The addition operation is referred to as "push," and the deletion operation as "pop." The most and least accessible elements in a stack are known as the top and bottom of the stack, respectively. Since insertion and deletion operations are performed at the end of a stack, the element can only be removed in the opposite order from that in which they were added to the stack. This is referred to as the discipline, and is the last item inserted is the first item deleted (LIFO). A stack is detailed in Figure 1.

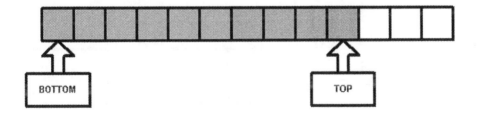

Figure 1. Linear Stack

Algorithm P inserts an element K into a stack S.

Algorithm P. Push an Element K into a Stack S.
The stack index is TOP. S has n available slots to store elements.
P1. [Overflow: Is the stack full?] if TOP ≥ n {print overflow message; exit;}
P2. [Increment TOP] TOP = TOP + 1;
P3. [Insert element into the stack.] S[TOP] = K; exit;

Algorithm D deletes an element from the stack S and returns the element deleted in a variable K.

Algorithm D. Pop an Element K from a Stack S
The stack index is TOP.
D1. [Underflow: Is an element in the stack?] if TOP ≤ 0 {print underflow message; exit;}
D2. [Un-stack an element or POP the stack.] K = S[TOP];
D3. [Decrement the stack index.] TOP = TOP – 1; exit;

2.2. Queues

Another important linear structure of variable size is the queue. A queue permits deletions at one end and additions at the other. The information is processed in the same order as it was received. The discipline is first item in is the first item out (FIFO) or a first-come, first-served (FCFS) operation. This type of structure is called a queue. Items are inserted into the rear and deletions are taken from the front. A queue is detailed in Figure 2.

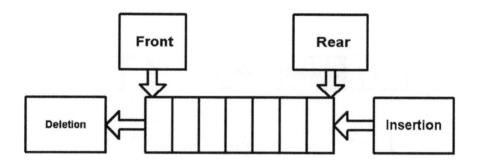

Figure 2. Linear Queue

Algorithm I inserts an element K into a queue Q.

Algorithm I. Insert an Element K into a Queue Q
Given values indexes F for front and R for rear elements of queue Q. Initially F and R have been set to a value of zero. There are slots for n elements in the queue.
I1. [Overflow: Is Q full?] if $R \geq n$ {print overflow message; exit;}
I2. [Increment the rear index] $R = R + 1$;
I3. [Insert the element K into the queue.] $Q[R] = K$;
I4. [Is the front index F properly set?] if $F = 0$ {$F = 1$; exit}

Algorithm J. deletes an element from the queue and returns it in K.

Algorithm J. Delete an Element from a Queue Q
The element deleted from the queue is stored in K.
J1. [Underflow: Is the queue empty?] if $F = 0$ {print underflow message; exit;}
J2. [Delete an element from the queue.] $K = Q[F]$;
J3. [Increment the front queue index.] $F = F + 1$; exit;

2.3. Deques

A deque is a special queue in which insertions and deletions are made from either the front or the rear of the queue. Operations on a deque are insert front, insert rear, delete front, and delete rear.

3. Java Utilities Package and Bit Manipulation

3.1. Class Vector of Package java.util

The Vector class enables us to create array-like objects that can grow and shrink dynamically as a program's data storage requirements change. In most programming languages, conventional arrays detailed in [10] are fixed in size. Arrays cannot grow or shrink in response to an application's changing storage requirements. Java Vector class allows array-like data structures that can dynamically resize themselves.

The amount of space reserved for an array is called its capacity. A Vector contains a number of elements which is less than or equal to its capacity. A vector grows by an increment that the programmer specifies or by default assumed by the system. If no capacity increment is specified, the system will automatically double the size of the Vector each time additional capacity is needed. Figure 3 details an assignment of student grades application that uses many class Vector methods. Student scores are stored on an input device. Student scores are read and stored in a Vector. The student scores are retrieved from the Vector and the best score is used as a base to assign letter grades. The assignment of student grades application is detailed with a range of steps:

1. The class AssignGrade that include Ibuf, Inf, and readDouble assigns student grades.

```
import java.util.*;
import javax.swing.*;
import java.io.*;
public class AssignGrade
{ //--------------------------------------------------
  // Setup File Reference Handle for File Name
  //--------------------------------------------------
```

```
public static BufferedReader Ibuf (String filename)
throws java.io.IOException
{
  // Setup the basic input stream
  FileReader fr = new FileReader (filename);
  // Buffer the input stream
  BufferedReader br = new BufferedReader (fr);
  return br;
} // End Ibuf
  //--------------------
// Input a Data Item
//--------------------
public static String Inf (BufferedReader br)
throws java.io.IOException
{ String inval;
  if ((inval = br.readLine ( )) != null)
    {
      return inval;
    } else return null;

} // End Inf
// ----------------------------------------------------
// Read a double value from the input device
// ----------------------------------------------------
public static double readDouble (BufferedReader HL)
throws java.io.IOException
{ String tval;
  tval = Inf (HL);
  if (tval == null) return -1.00;
  else return Double.parseDouble (tval);
} // End readDouble
// ----------------
// main method
// ----------------
public static void main(String [ ] args)
throws java.io.IOException
{
```

2. Define a vector container dataVector. This application requires that storage be allocated and managed for a number of students that are not known at program translation time. A vector container is ideal for this application.

```
Vector dataVector = new Vector ( ); // Vector to hold scores
double best = 0; // The best score
char grade; // The grade
```

3. Display a dialog box to the user and request a path and file name for the student data.

```
String Fname = " "; // Input file name
// Input the grade file path and name
Fname = JOptionPane.showInputDialog ("Enter the Path and"+
"FileName");
```

4. Read the student data from an input device.

```
BufferedReader HT = Ibuf (Fname);
// Read scores and find the best score
// An empty input device file terminates input
do
{
  // Read a score from the input device
  double score = readDouble (HT);
  // End of file on negative score
  if (score < 0) break;
```

5. Store each student data object read in a vector called dataVector.

```
  // Add the score into the vector
  dataVector.addElement (new Double (score));
  // Find the best score
  if (score > best)
    best = score;
} while (true);
```

6. Assign student grades and produce an output report.

```
JOptionPane.showMessageDialog (null, "Total Number of Students"
+dataVector.size ( ));
// Assign and display grades
for (int i = 0; i < dataVector.size ( ); i++)
```

```
    {
      // Retrieve an element from the vector
      Double studentScore = (Double)(dataVector.elementAt (i));
      // Get the score and assign a grade
      double score = studentScore.doubleValue ( );
      if (score >= (best – 10))
        grade = 'A';
      else if (score >= (best – 20))
        grade = 'B';
      else if (score >= (best – 30))
        grade = 'C';
      else if (score >= (best – 40))
        grade = 'D';
      else
        grade = 'F';
      // Output the student number, score, and grade
      System.out.println ("Student" +i + "score is" +score+
      "and grade is" +grade);
    } // End for
  } // End main
} // End class AssignGrade
```

Figure 3. Assign Student Grades Using class Vector

Vector Class Information is detailed in Appendix C. Figure 3 details an implementation that assigns an undetermined but finite number of student grades to scores read from an input device. The scores are stored in a Vector as Double objects. A Vector is allocated called dataVector with a Vector Class constructor using Vector dataVector = new Vector ( );. Convert each score to a Double object and store them in the allocated Vector dataVector with dataVector.addElement (new Double (score));. Retrieve each object from the Vector dataVector with the statements Double studentScore = (Double)(dataVector.elementAt (i)); and double score = studentScore.doubleValue ( );.

The number of student scores is not known at program design and compile time. The Vector data structure dynamically allocates storage at run time for data storage. This data structure meets the application requirement without excessive programmer storage management to meet the application storage requirements. Programming error is reduced by using a few methods from the Vector Class to implement the application.

3.2. Class Stack of Package java.util

In Chapter 2, "Data Structures," we learned how to build fundamental data structures such as stacks, queues, and deques. Java offers data structures in classes. These data structures are located in the Java utilities package java.util.

The Vector class implements a dynamically resizable array. Class Stack extends class Vector to implement a stack data structure. Class Stack is designed to store objects. Primitive data types must be type-wrapped to store as Stack objects. The wrapper class for primitive data types are Boolean, Byte, Character, Short, Integer, Long, Float, and Double. Selected Stack methods are detailed in Figure 4. Student scores are stored on an input device. Student scores are read and stored in a Stack. The student scores are retrieved from the Stack and the best score is used as a base to assign letter grades. The assign student grades application using a stack is detailed with a range of steps:

1. The class AssignGradeStack that include Ibuf, Inf, and readDouble assigns student grades.

```
import java.util.*;
import javax.swing.*;
import java.io.*;
public class AssignGradeStack
{ //----------------------------------------------------
 // Setup File Reference Handle for File Name
 //----------------------------------------------------
 public static BufferedReader Ibuf (String filename)
 throws java.io.IOException
 {
  // Setup the basic input stream
  FileReader fr = new FileReader (filename);
  // Buffer the input stream
  BufferedReader br = new BufferedReader (fr);
  return br;
 } // End Ibuf
 //----------------------
 // Input a Data Item
 //----------------------
 public static String Inf (BufferedReader br)
 throws java.io.IOException
```

```
{ String inval;
  if ((inval = br.readLine ( )) != null)
   {
     return inval;
   } else return null;
 } // End Inf


// ---------------------------------------------------
// Read a double value from the input device
// ---------------------------------------------------
public static double readDouble (BufferedReader HL)
throws java.io.IOException
{ String tval;
  tval = Inf (HL);
  if (tval == null) return -1.00;
  else return Double.parseDouble (tval);
} // End readDouble
// ----------------
// main method
// ----------------
public static void main (String [ ] args)
throws java.io.IOException
 {
```

2. Define a stack container dataStack. This application requires that storage be allocated and managed for a number of students that are not known at program translation time. A stack container allocated using a Stack constructor from the java.util package is ideal for this application.

```
    Stack dataStack = new Stack ( ); // Stack to hold scores
    double best = 0; // The best score
    char grade; // The grade
    int i = 0; // An integer variable
```

3. Display a dialog box to the user and request a path and file name for the student data.

```
    String Fname = " "; // Input file name
    // Input the grade file path and name
    Fname = JOptionPane.showInputDialog ("Enter the Path and"+
    "FileName");
```

```
BufferedReader HT = Ibuf (Fname);
// Read scores and find the best score
// An empty input device file terminates input
do
{
```

4. Read the student data from an input device.

```
// Read a score from the input device
double score = readDouble (HT);
// End of file on negative score
if (score < 0) break;
```

5. Store each student data object read in a stack called dataStack.

```
// Add the score into the Stack
dataStack.push (new Double (score));
// Find the best score
if (score > best)
  best = score;
} while (true);
```

6. Assign student grades and produce an output report.

```
JOptionPane.showMessageDialog (null, "Total Number of Students"
+dataStack.size ( ));
// Assign and display grades
i = dataStack.size ( );
// Assign and display grades
while (!dataStack.isEmpty ( ))
{
  // Retrieve an element from the Stack
  Double doubleObject = (Double)(dataStack.pop ( ));
  // Get the score
  double score = doubleObject.doubleValue ( );
  // Assign a letter grade
  if (score >= best – 10)
    grade = 'A';
  else if (score >= best – 20)
    grade = 'B';
  else if (score >= best – 30)
    grade = 'C';
```

```
    else if (score >= best – 40)
      grade = 'D';
    else
      grade = 'F';
    // Output student index, score, and letter grade
    System.out.println ("Student" + i-- + "score is" + score +
    "and grade is" + grade);
   } // End while
  } // End main
} // End class AssignGradeStack
```
Figure 4. Assign Student Grades Using class Stack

3.3. Class Hashtable

We are given a key K, for a record and a key-to-address or index transformation, that generates an address or index used in the storage or retrieval of that record in a table. We use the term bucket as that area in a table where records are stored. The bucked size is the maximum number of records that can be contained in a bucket. A bucket can be thought of as being divided into slots. Each slot is designed to hold one data record. Therefore, the ratio of the active keys to the total slots available in all buckets is called the load factor.

A key-to-address transformation h(K), sometimes called a hashing function, maps from the key space into the bucket address space. We want h(K) to give a uniform random distribution while mapping K into the bucket addresses. After generating an address h(K) the address is used to enter the address space. This entering of the address space with h(K) is called probing. When the same h(K) is used to enter the address space more than one time, the sequence is called a probe sequence.

The address h(K), where K is the key, is called the home address. Distinct keys mapped into the same bucket slot are called synonyms. Such an occurrence is called a collision at the home address. If a one-to-one map can be constructed then the function is said to be a direct addressing function. When the number of records in a bucket exceeds the bucket size we have an overflow. In many cases the overflow records are kept in a common area called an overflow area. The overflow area is typically a linked list of all key/value pairs that hash to that cell in the hashtable. This is the solution that Java's Hashtable class implements. There are many hashing methods. Hashing methods are detailed in [2, 9]. The application in Figure 5 details selected Hashtable class methods. A. selected hash methods application is detailed with a range of steps:

1. Start a class HashAll with a method called hall that use selected methods from the java.util package to store and retrieve data in a hash table.

```
import java.util.*;
import java.awt.*;
import java.awt.event.*;
import javax.swing.*;
public class HashAll
{ // Setup a Hash Table Object
```

2. Define a Hashtable container table. This application requires that storage be allocated and managed for a number of students that are not known at program translation time. A Hashtable container allocated using a Hashtable constructor from the java.util package is ideal for this application.

```
public Hashtable table = new Hashtable ( );
public String fname, lname, cnt;
// Hash Table Operation Method
```

3. Display a dialog box of program options for user input.

```
public void hall ( )
{ int j;
  StringBuffer buf = new StringBuffer ( );
  do
  {
  cnt = JOptionPane.showInputDialog ("Enter Control Code\nCode
  Operation\n1      Insert\n2      Get Key\n3      Remove
  Key\n4      Empty Table\n5      Contains Key\n6
  Clear Table\n7      List Objects\n8      List Keys\n9
  Greater Than 8 Stop ");
  j = Integer.parseInt(cnt);
  // Is it an insert, remove key, or contains key?
  if ((j == 1) || (j == 2) || (j == 3) || (j == 5))
    { fname = JOptionPane.showInputDialog ("Enter First Name");
      lname = JOptionPane.showInputDialog ("Enter Last Name (Key)");
    }
  Object val;
```

4. User selected options put an object in the hash table, get an object from the hash table, remove an object from the hash table, clear the hash table, list objects, and list keys.

```
switch (j)
{
case 1: // Insert Key
        val = table.put (lname, fname);
        if (val == null)
        JOptionPane.showMessageDialog (null, "Put:" +
        fname,"HashTable", JOptionPane.PLAIN_MESSAGE);
        else
        JOptionPane.showMessageDialog (null, "Put:" + fname+
            "; Replaced:" + val.toString ( ), "HashTable",
        JOptionPane.PLAIN_MESSAGE);
        break;
case 2: // Get Key
        val = table.get (lname);
        if (val != null)
        JOptionPane.showMessageDialog (null, "Get:" +
        val.toString ( ), "HashTable", JOptionPane.PLAIN_MESSAGE);
        else
        JOptionPane.showMessageDialog (null, "Get:" + lname+
        "not in table","HashTable", JOptionPane.PLAIN_MESSAGE);
        break;
case 3: // Remove Key
        val = table.remove (lname);
        if (val != null)
        JOptionPane.showMessageDialog (null, "Remove:" +
        val.toString ( ),"HashTable", JOptionPane.PLAIN_MESSAGE);
        else
        JOptionPane.showMessageDialog (null, "Remove:" + lname+
        "not in table","HashTable",JOptionPane.PLAIN_MESSAGE);
        break;
case 4: // Empty Table
        JOptionPane.showMessageDialog (null, "Empty:" +
        table.isEmpty ( ),"HashTable",JOptionPane.PLAIN_MESSAGE);
        break;
case 5: // Contains Key
        JOptionPane.showMessageDialog (null, "Contains key:"
```

```
              +lname+ " " + table.containsKey (lname), "HashTable",
              JOptionPane.PLAIN_MESSAGE);
              break;
      case 6: //Clear Table
              table.clear ( );
              JOptionPane.showMessageDialog (null, "Clear: Table is
              now empty", "HashTable", JOptionPane.PLAIN_MESSAGE);
              break;
      case 7: // List Objects
              for (Enumeration num = table.elements ( );
              num.hasMoreElements ( );)
                buf.append(num.nextElement ( )).append('\n');
              JOptionPane.showMessageDialog (null,"List of Objects: "
              +buf.toString ( ),"HashTable",JOptionPane.PLAIN_MESSAGE);
              break;
      case 8: // List Keys
              for (Enumeration enum1 = table.keys ( );
              num.hasMoreElements ( );)
                buf.append (num.nextElement ( )).append ('\n');
              // Display the List of Keys
              JOptionPane.showMessageDialog (null, buf.toString ( ),
              "Hash Table", JOptionPane.PLAIN_MESSAGE);
              break;
      } // End Switch
  } while (j < 9);  // End do while
  } // End Method hall
  // ----------------
  // main method
  // ----------------
  public static void main (String args [ ])
  {
    HashAll app = new HashAll ( );
    app.hall ( );
  } // End main
} // End class HashAll
```
Figure 5. Selected Hashtable Methods

The HashTable application in Figure 5 implements several HashTable Class methods from Figure 6 and Figure 7. A constructor from Figure 6 creates a container using the statement public Hashtable table = new Hashtable ( );. The statement val = table. put (lname, fname); from Figure 7 inserts a key into the HashTable. Retrieve a key from the HashTable with val = table.get (lname);. Remove a key from the HashTable with
val = table.remove (lname);. Check for the existence of a key in the Hash
Table with table.containsKey (lname). Clear the HashTable with table.clear ( );.

Method Name	Description
Hashtable( )	Constructs a new, empty hashtable with a default initial capacity (11) and load factor, which is 0.75.
Hashtable(int initialCapacity)	Constructs a new, empty hashtable with the specified initial capacity and default load factor, which is 0.75.
Hashtable(int initialCapacity, float loadFactor)	Constructs a new, empty hashtable with the specified initial capacity and the specified l o a d factor.
Hashtable(Map<? ? extends V> t)	extends K, Constructs a new hashtable with the same mappings as the given Map.

Figure 6. HashTable Class Constructor Summary
Note: This is a modification of selected information from [14].

Type	Method Name	Description
void	clear ( )	Clears this hashtable so that it contains no keys.
Object	clone ( )	Creates a shallow copy of this hashtable.
boolean	contains (Object value)	Tests if some key maps into the specified value in this hashtable.

boolean	containsKey (Object key)	Tests if the specified object is a key in this hashtable.
boolean	containsValue (Object value)	Returns true if this Hashtable maps one or more keys to this value.
Enumeration	elements ( )	Returns an enumeration of the values in this hashtable.
Set	<Map.Entry<K,V>> entrySet( )	Returns a Set view of the entries contained in this Hashtable.
boolean	equals (Object o)	Compares the specified Object with this Map for equality, as per the definition in the Map interface.
V	get (Object key)	Returns the value to which the specified key is mapped in this hashtable.
int	hashCode ( )	Returns the hash code value for this Map as per the definition in the Map interface.
boolean	isEmpty( )	Tests if this hashtable maps no keys to values.
Enumeration<K>	keys ( )	Returns an enumeration of the keys in this hashtable.
Set<K>	keySet ( )	Returns a Set view of the keys contained in this Hashtable.
V	put (K key, V value)	Maps the specified key to the specified value in this hashtable.
void	putAll (Map<? extends K,? extends V> t)	Copies all of the mappings from the specified Map to this Hashtable These mappings will replace any mappings that this Hashtable had for any of the keys currently in the specified Map.

protected	void	rehash ( ) Increases the capacity of and internally reorganizes this hashtable, in order to accommodate and access its entries more efficiently.
V	remove (Object key)	Removes the key (and its Corresponding value) from this hashtable.
int	size ( )	Returns the number of keys in this hashtable.
String	toString ( )	Returns a string representation of this Hashtable object in the form of a set of entries, enclosed in braces and separated by the ASCII characters "," (comma and space).
Collection<V>	values ( )	Returns a Collection view of the values contained in this Hashtable.

Figure 7. HashTable Class Method Summary
Note: This is a modification of selected information from [14].

3.4. Class Properties

A Properties object is a persistent Hashtable object. Persistence is the concept that an object can exist separate from the executing program that creates it. Java contains a mechanism called object serialization for creating persistent objects. When an object is serialized, it is transformed into a sequence of bits; this sequence is serialized, it is transformed into a sequence of bytes; this sequence is a raw binary representation of the object. A Persistence object can be written to an output stream and directed to a file, then read back in through an input stream. Class Properties selected methods are detailed in Figure 8. A. selected class properties application is detailed with a range of steps:

1. Start a class PropertiesCheck with methods listProperties and PropertiesSelect.
```
import java.io.*;
import java.util.*;
import java.awt.*;
```

```
import java.awt.event.*;
import javax.swing.*;
// Selected class Properties
public class PropertiesCheck
{
    private Properties table = new Properties ( );
    // List properties
```

2. Create a list of properties and display them in a message dialog box.

```
    public void listProperties ( )
    throws java.io.IOException
    {
        StringBuffer buf = new StringBuffer ( );
        String pkey, pval;
        Enumeration num = table.propertyNames ( );
        while (num.hasMoreElements ( ))
        {
            pkey = num.nextElement ( ).toString ( );
            pval = table.getProperty (pkey);
            buf.append (pkey).append ('\t');
            buf.append (" ").append ('\t');
            buf.append (pval).append ('\n');
        }
        JOptionPane.showMessageDialog (null, buf ,"List Properties",
        JOptionPane.PLAIN_MESSAGE);
    } // End listProperties
```

3. Implement a method PropertiesSelect that uses class Properties methods put, clear, get property, save, and load. Receive input to select the properties from an input dialog box. Display the results in a message dialog box.

```
    // class Properties put, clear, get property, save, and load
    public void PropertiesSelect ( )
    throws java.io.IOException
    {
        Object val;
        String pval = " ";
        String pkey = " ";
        String cnt = " ";
        int j;
```

```
do
{
    // Input a class Property control code
    cnt = JOptionPane.showInputDialog ("Enter Control Code\nCode  Operation\n1
    Put\n2        Clear\n3        Get Property\n4        Save\n5        Load\n6
    Greater Than 6 Stop");
    j = Integer.parseInt (cnt);
    // Check for the Stop code
    if (j > 5) break;
    // Execute the control code
    switch (j)
    {
    case 1: // Put
            pval = JOptionPane.showInputDialog ("Property value");
            pkey = JOptionPane.showInputDialog ("Property name (key)");
            val = table.put (pkey, pval);
            if (pval == null)
                JOptionPane.showMessageDialog (null, "Put:" + pkey + " " + pval ,
                "class" +
                "Properties Example", JOptionPane.PLAIN_MESSAGE);
            else
                JOptionPane.showMessageDialog (null, "Put:" + pkey + " " + pval+
                "; Replaced:" + val, "class Properties Example",
                JOptionPane.PLAIN_MESSAGE);
            listProperties ( );
            break;
    case 2: // Clear
            table.clear ( );
            JOptionPane.showMessageDialog (null, "Table in memory cleared" ,
            "class Properties Example", JOptionPane.PLAIN_MESSAGE);
            listProperties ( );
            break;
    case 3: // Get property
            val = table.getProperty (pkey);
            if (val != null)
                JOptionPane.showMessageDialog (null, "Get property:" + pkey + " " +
                val ,"class Properties Example", JOptionPane.PLAIN_MESSAGE);
            else
                JOptionPane.showMessageDialog (null, "Get:" + pkey + "not in table" ,
```

```
            "class Properties Example", JOptionPane.PLAIN_MESSAGE);
            listProperties ( );
            break;
    case 4: // Save
            try
              {
              FileOutputStream output;
              output = new FileOutputStream ("props.dat");
              table.store (output, "Sample Properties");
              output.close ( );
              listProperties ( );
              }
            Catch (IOException ex)
                {
                JOptionPane.showMessageDialog  (null,  ex.toString  ( ),  "class
                Properties"+
                "Example", JOptionPane.PLAIN_MESSAGE);
                }
            break;

    case 5: // Load
            try
              {
              FileInputStream input;
              input = new FileInputStream ("props.dat");
              table.load (input);
              input.close ( );
              listProperties ( );
              }
            Catch (IOException ex)
                {
                JOptionPane.showMessageDialog (null, ex.toString ( ) , "class"+
                "Properties Example", JOptionPane.PLAIN_MESSAGE);
                }
            break;
      } // End Switch
     } while (j < 6); // End do while
    } // End PropertiesSelect
   // ----------------
```

```
// main method
// ---------------
public static void main (String args [ ])
throws java.io.IOException
{
  PropertiesCheck app = new PropertiesCheck ( );
  app.PropertiesSelect ( );
} // End main
} // End PropertiesCheck
```
Figure 8. Selected class Properties of the java.util Package

Properties value and name are input in a GUI dialog box using

```
pval = JOptionPane.showInputDialog ("Property value");
pkey = JOptionPane.showInputDialog ("Property name (key)");
```

The properties input are stored in a properties table with the statement val = table. put (pkey, pval);. The properties table is cleared with table.clear ( );. Properties are retrieved from the properties table with val = table.getProperty (pkey);. Figure 8 detailed an implementation that used methods from the Properties class. Properties class constructors are detailed in Figure 9 and other Properties class methods are detailed in Figure 10.

Method Name	Description
Properties ( )	Creates an empty property list with no default values.
Properties (Properties defaults)	Creates an empty property list with the specified defaults.

Figure 9. Properties Class Constructor Summary
Note: This is a modification of the information in [14].

Type	Method Name	Description
String	getProperty (String key)	Searches for the property with the specified key in this property list.

String	getProperty (String key, String defaultValue)	Searches for the property with the specified key in this property list.
void	list (PrintStream out)	Prints this property list out to the specified output stream.
void	list (PrintWriter out)	Prints this property list out to the specified output stream.
void	load (InputStream inStream)	Reads a property list (key and element pairs) from the input stream.
void	loadFromXML (InputStream in)	Loads all of the properties represented by the XML document on the specified input stream into this properties table.
Enumeration	propertyNames ( )	Returns an enumeration of all the keys in this property list, including distinct keys in the default property list if a key of the same name has not already been found from the main properties list.
void	save (OutputStream out, String comments)	Deprecated. This method does not throw an IOException if an I/O error occurs while saving the property list. The preferred way to save a properties list is via the store(OutputStream out, String comments) method or the storeToXML(OutputStream os, String comment) method.
Object	setProperty (String key, String value)	Calls the Hashtable method put.

void	store (OutputStream out, String comments)	Writes this property list (key and element pairs) in this Properties table to the output stream in a format suitable for loading into a Properties table using the load method.
void	storeToXML (OutputStream os, String comment)	Emits an XML document representing all of the properties contained in this table.
void	storeToXML (OutputStream os, String comment, String encoding)	Emits an XML document representing all of the properties contained in this table, using the specified encoding.

Figure 10. Properties Class Method Summary
Note: This is a modification of selected information from [14].

3.5. Class BitSet and Bitwise Operators

3.5.1. Class BitSet

This is class in java.util. BitSet defines an arbitrary large set of bits. Instance methods allow you to set, clear, and query individual bits in the set, and also to perform bitwise Boolean arithmetic on the bits in BitSet objects. This class can be used as an extremely compact array of Boolean values, although reading and writing those values is slower than normal array access.

Each component of the bit set has a boolean value. The bits of a BitSet are indexed by nonnegative integers. Individual indexed bits can be examined, set, or cleared. One BitSet may be used to modify the contents of another BitSet through logical AND, logical inclusive OR, and logical exclusive OR operations. By default, all bits in the set initially have the value false.

Every bit set has a current size, which is the number of bits of space currently in use by the bit set. Note that the size is related to the implementation of a bit set, so it may change with implementation. The length of a bit set relates to logical length of a bit set and is defined independently of implementation. Selected Java BitSet class methods are detailed in Figure 11 that performs Sieve of Eratosthenes. A selected class BitSet application is detailed with a range of steps:

1. Start a class BitSetAll with a method BGetSetGen to perform Stieve of Eratosthenes.

```
import java.awt.*;
import java.awt.event.*;
import java.util.*;
import javax.swing.*;
public class BitSetAll
{
```

2. Allocate a BitSet container sieve using a BitSet constructor. Perform the Sieve of Eratosthenes using selected methods from the BitSet class.

```
public BitSet sieve = new BitSet (1024);
public void BitSetGen ( )
{ String bval;
  int val, bound, i, j, lastBit, counter;
  // Set all bits from 1 to 1023
  bound = sieve.size ( );
  for (i = 1; i < bound; i++)
    sieve.set (i);
  // Perform Sieve of Eratosthenes
  lastBit = (int) Math.sqrt (sieve.size ( ));
  for (i = 2; i < lastBit; i++)
    if (sieve.get (i))
      for (j = 2 * i; j < bound; j += i)
        sieve.clear (j);
  counter = 0;
  for (i = 1; i < bound; i++)
    if (sieve.get (i))
      {
        System.out.print (String.valueOf (i));
        System.out.print (++counter % 7 == 0 ? "\n" : "\t");
      }
```

```
do
{
```

3. Receive input from the user with an input dialog box. Output the outcome for the input in a message dialog box.

```
bval = JOptionPane.showInputDialog ("Enter a value from " +"1 to 1023 or"+
   "Negative to Stop");
val = Integer.parseInt (bval);
if (val < 0) break;
if (sieve.get (val))
   JOptionPane.showMessageDialog (null, val + "is a prime number" , "BitSet "+
   "Example", JOptionPane.PLAIN_MESSAGE);
else
   JOptionPane.showMessageDialog (null, val + "is not a prime number",
   "BitSet Example", JOptionPane.PLAIN_MESSAGE);
} while (val > 0); // End do while
} // End BitSetGen
// ---------------
// main method
// ---------------
public static void main (String args [ ])
{
   BitSetAll app = new BitSetAll ( );
   app.BitSetGen ( );
} // End main
} // End BitAll
```
Figure 11. Using a BitSet to Demonstrate the Sieve of Eratosthenes

The BitSet class constructor public BitSet sieve = new BitSet (1024); creates the container sieve. BitSet constructors are detailed in Figure 12. Other BitSet class methods bound = sieve.size ( );, sieve.set (i);, sieve.get (i)), sieve.clear (j); are detailed in Figure 13.

Method Name	Description
BitSet ( )	Creates a new bit set.
BitSet (int nbits)	Creates a bit set whose initial size is large enough to explicitly represent bits with indices in the range 0 through nbits-1.

Figure 12. BitSet Constructor Summary

Type	Method Name	Description
void	and (BitSet set)	Performs a logical AND of this target bit set with the argument bit set.
void	andNot (BitSet set)	Clears all of the bits in this BitSet whose corresponding bit is set in the specified BitSet.
int	cardinality ( ) to true in	Returns the number of bits set this BitSet.
void	clear ( )	Sets all of the bits in this BitSet to false.
void	clear (int bitIndex)	Sets the bit specified by the index to false.
void	clear (int fromIndex, int toIndex)	Sets the bits from the specified fromIndex(inclusive) to the specified toIndex(exclusive) to false.
Object	clone ( )	Cloning this BitSet produces a new BitSet that is equal to it.
boolean	equals (Object obj)	Compares this object against the specified object.
void	flip (int bitIndex)	Sets the bit at the specified index to the complement of its current value.
void	flip (int fromIndex, int toIndex)	Sets each bit from the specified fromIndex(inclusive) to the specified toIndex(exclusive) to the complement of its current value.

boolean	get (int bitIndex)	Returns the value of the bit with the specified index.
BitSet	get (int fromIndex, int toIndex)	Returns a new BitSet composed of bits from this BitSet from fromIndex(inclusive) to toIndex (exclusive).
int	hashCode ( )	Returns a hash code value for this bit set.
boolean	intersects (BitSet set)	Returns true if the specified BitSet has any bits set to true that are also set to true in this BitSet.
boolean	isEmpty ( )	Returns true if this BitSet contains no bits that are set to true.
int	length ( )	Returns the "logical size" of this BitSet: the index of the highest set bit in the BitSet plus one.
int	nextClearBit (int fromIndex)	Returns the index of the first bit that is set to false that occurs on or after the specified starting index.
int	nextSetBit (int fromIndex)	Returns the index of the first bit that is set to true that occurs on or after the specified starting index.
void	or (BitSet set)	Performs a logical OR of this bit set with the bit set argument.
void	set (int bitIndex)	Sets the bit at the specified index to true.
void	set (int bitIndex, boolean value)	Sets the bit at the specified index to the specified value.

void	set (int fromIndex, int toIndex)	Sets the bits from the specified fromIndex (inclusive) to the specified toIndex (exclusive) to true.
void	set (int fromIndex, boolean value)	Sets the bits from the specified fromIndex(inclusive) to the specified toIndex (exclusive) to the specified value.
int	size ( )	Returns the number of bits of space actually in use by this BitSet to represent bit values.
String	toString ( )	Returns a string representation of this bit set.
void	xor (BitSet set)	Performs a logical XOR of this bit set with the bit set argument.

Figure 13. BitSet Class Method Summary
Note: This is a modification of the information in [14].

3.5.2. Bitwise Operators

Java bitwise operators are detailed in Figure 14

Bitwise Operator	Description
<< Left shift	x << y is the value obtained by shifting the bits in x y positions to the left
>> Right shift with sign extension	x >> y is the value obtained by shifting the bits in x positions to the right
>>> Right shift with zero extension	--
& Bitwise AND	b_1 & b_2 is 1 if both b_1 and b_2 or both are 1; it is zero otherwise
| Bitwise OR	b_1 | b_2 is 1 if either b_1 or b_2 or both are 1; it is 0
Otherwise $\wedge$ Bitwise EXCLUSIVE OR	b_1 $\wedge$ b_2 is 1 if exactly one of b_1 or b_2 is 1; it is 0

otherwise
~ Complement (invert all bits)   ~b is 0 if b is 1; ~b is 1 if b is 0
Figure 14. Java Bitwise Operators

The left shift moves all bits to the left, filling in zeros in the least significant bits. Shifting to the left by n bits yields the same result as multiplication by 2^n. The arithmetic right shift moves all bits to the right, propagating the sign bit. Therefore, the result is the same as integer division by 2^n?, both for positive and negative values. Finally, the bitwise right shift moves all bits to the right, filling in zeros in the most significant bits.

3.6. Exercises

1. Implement an algorithm as a method to load a hash table. Load the information from a hard disk file called HAS.DAT into the table H. The data stored as one number per record in HAS.DAT are 32, 18, 20, 10, 226, 172, 50, 456, 691, 30, 100, 80, 340, 234, 349, 986, 234, 198, 275, and 384. HAS.DAT has 20 data items; however, the input must be designed for an unknown number of items.

2. Implement an algorithm as methods to search for keys from the hard disk file KEY.DAT in table H. The data stored as one number per record in KEY.DAT are 2, 691, 234, 1000, 10. KEY.DAT has 5 data items; however, the input must be designed for an unknown number of items. Post all the output in one GUI dialog box as sentences with one key per line.

3. Integrate the methods in problems one and two into one GUI to operate the load and search operations on a hash table.

4. Insert code in the AssignStudentGrades class in Figure 3 that implements the add, addall, capacity, clear, clone, contains, containsAll, copyInfo, ensureCapacity, firstElement, get, hashCode, indexOf, insertElementAt, isEmpty, lastElement, lastIndexOf, remove, removeAll, set, setsize, toArray, and trimToSize methods described in Appendix C.

5. Insert code in the HashAll class in Figure 5 that implements the contains, containsValue, entrySet, keySet, and values methods described in Figure 6 and Figure 7.

6. Insert code in the PropertiesChack class in Figure 8 that implements the list and setProperty methods described in Figure 9 and Figure 10.

7. Insert code in the BitSetAll class in Figure 11 that implements the cardinality, clone, equals, flip, hashCode, isempty, length, nextClearBit, nextSetBit, and toString methods described in Figure 13.

4. Selected Collections

A collection sometimes called a container is an object that groups multiple elements into a single unit. Collections are used to store, retrieve, manipulate, and communicate aggregate data. Selected members are explained in this textbook to illustrate the use of collections. Collection class member's use is driven by the application requirements. The aim is to point to the members in the Collection and give an example of the implementation of a subset of the members in a manner that implicitly applies to other members. The selected members detailed in this textbook are Lists, HashSet, SortedSets and TreeSets, and Queue. Many methods of the Collection class are defined in Appendix C called Class Vector Information.

A Java collections framework is a unified architecture for representing and manipulating collections. All collections frameworks contain the following:

Interfaces: These are abstract data types that represent collections. Interfaces allow collections to be manipulated independently of the details of their representation. In object-oriented languages, interfaces generally form a hierarchy.
Implementations: These are the concrete implementations of the collection interfaces as reusable data structures.

Algorithms: These are the methods that perform useful computations, such as searching and sorting, on objects that implement collection interfaces. The algorithms are said to be polymorphic: that is, the same method can be used on many different implementations of the appropriate collection interface. In essence, algorithms are reusable functionality.

The Java Collections Framework provides the following benefits:

Reduces programming effort: By providing useful data structures and algorithms, the Collections Framework frees you to concentrate on the important parts of your program rather than on the low-level "plumbing" required to make it work.

Increases program speed and quality: This Collections Framework provides high-performance, high-quality implementations of useful data structures and algorithms. The various implementations of each interface are interchangeable, so programs can be easily tuned by switching collection implementations.

Allows interoperability among unrelated Application Program Interfaces (APIs): The collection interfaces are the paths by which APIs pass collections back and forth. Reduces effort to learn and to use new APIs: Many APIs naturally take collections on input and furnish them as output. With the advent of standard collection interfaces, learned information can be ported from the use of one data structure to another.

Reduces effort to design new APIs: This is the flip side of the previous advantage. Designers and implementers don't have to reinvent the wheel each time they create an API that relies on collections; instead they can use standard collection interfaces. Fosters software reuse: New data structures that conform to the standard collection interfaces and algorithms that operate on objects that implement these interfaces are reusable.

The selected collection interfaces encapsulate different types of collections, which are detailed in Figure 15. These interfaces allow collections to be manipulated independently of the details of their representation.

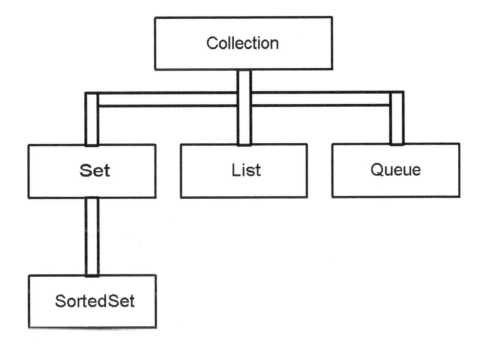

Figure 15. Selected Collections Interfaces.

A Set is a special kind of Collection, a SortedSet is a special kind of Set. A List and a Queue is a special kind of collection.

4.1. Using Lists and ListIterators

The user of an ordered collection interface has precise control over where in the list each element is inserted. The user can access elements by their integer index, and search for elements in the list. Unlike sets, lists typically allow duplicate elements. Lists typically allow pairs of elements e1 and e2 such that e1.equals(e2), and they typically allow multiple null elements. It is possible to implement a list that prohibits duplicates, by throwing runtime exceptions when the user attempts to insert duplicates.

The List interface places additional stipulations on the constructs of the iterator, add, remove, equals, and hashCode methods. The List interface provides four methods for positional indexed access to list elements. Lists are zero based.

The List interface provides a special iterator, called a ListIterator that allows element insertion and replacement, and bidirectional access in addition to the normal operations that the Iterator interface provides. A method is provided to obtain a list iterator that starts at a specified position in the list.

The List interface provides methods to search for a specified object.

The List interface provides methods to efficiently insert and remove multiple elements at an arbitrary point in the list.

Linked Lists, Linked Stacks, and Linked Queues are reviewed in Sections 4.1.1 through 4.1.3. The basic linked list processing data structures implementation steps are compared to the List Class implementation for the same data structures to point out the efficiencies of the use of the List Class methods.

4.1.1. Linked Lists

Instead of keeping a linear list in sequential memory locations, we can make use of a much more flexible scheme in which each node contains a link to the next node of the list. Define a variable whose content is the address or index of another location called a link variable or a pointer. Define a pointer to the linked allocation with a linked variable AVAIL. A linked allocation is detailed in Figure 16.

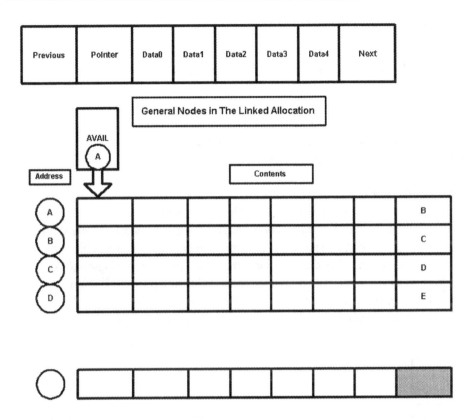

Figure 16. Linked Allocation With an Available Storage Pointer

In Figure 16, A, B, C, D, and E are arbitrary locations in memory, and shaded node is the null link. The link variable AVAIL points to the first node in the structure. The Next node of the structure contains the address or index to the next node in the structure. Other pointer nodes in the structure are Previous and Pointer. Data are stored as objects in the nodes Data0, Data1, .. , and Data4.

In a list processing (LISP) system the available storage pool is linked as the Next node is linked in Figure 16. A link variable points to the top of the storage pool. System operations are available to get a node from the pool, return a node to the pool, connect nodes using the link or Next node content, store data in nodes, retrieve data from nodes, and move from one node to another node. Linked list information is detailed in [9].

4.1.2. Linked Stacks

The direction of links for the stack is defined to facilitate easy insertion and deletion of nodes. A node can be added at the top or deleted one from the top.

We have already seen how to represent stacks and queues sequentially in Chapter 2. Such a representation proved efficient if we had only one stack in which we knew the maximum number of items at compile time. However, when several stacks and queues co-exist, there was no efficient way to represent them sequentially.

The operation of adding an object to the front of a linked list is quite similar to that of pushing an object onto a stack. In both cases, a new object is added as the only immediately accessible item in a collection. A stack can be accessed only through its top object, and lists can be accessed only from the pointer to its first object. Similarly, the operation of removing the first object from a linked list is analogous to popping a stack. In both cases, the only immediately accessible object of a collection is removed from that collection, and the next object becomes immediately accessible. We represent a linked stack by a linear linked list. A linked stack is detailed in Figure 17.

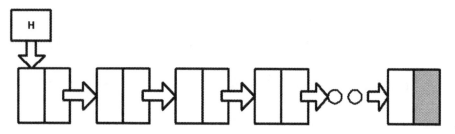

Figure 17. Linked Stack

Stacks are detailed in [9].

4.1.3. Linked Queues

The direction of links for the queue is defined to facilitate easy insertion and deletion of nodes. A node can be added at the rear and deletion can be performed at the front, for a queue. Objects are deleted from the front of a queue and inserted at the rear. Let the list pointer that points to the first object of a list represent the front of the queue. Another pointer to the last object of the list represents the front of the queue. A linked queue is detailed in Figure 18.

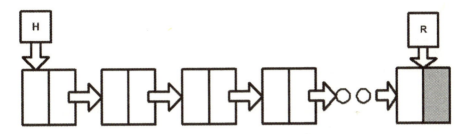

Figure 18. Linked Queue

Queue information is detailed in [9].

4.1.4. Selected Linked List Methods

Linked List methods are detailed in Figure 19. These methods load data into a linked list, concatenate linked list, insert a key in a linked list, search for a key in a linked list, remove a key from a linked list, insert an item in the front of a linked list, and insert an item in the rear of a linked list. A selected class List application is detailed with a range of steps:

1. The class ListTest uses methods from the List class to implement ListTest methods printList, loadListObject, loadListInt, locate, removeKey, addFront, addRear, insertKey, and conCat.
```
import java.util.*;
public class ListTest
{
    private String colors [ ] = { "black", "yellow", "green",
                    "blue", "violet", "silver" };
    private int num [ ] = { 10, 30, 60, 90, 100, 1024 };
    public ListTest ( )
    { String yell = "violet";
      String tell = "ed";
```

2. Allocate linked list containers link and link2 using the LinkedList constructor.
```
    LinkedList link = new LinkedList ( );
    LinkedList link2 = new LinkedList ( );
    int j;
```

3. Load objects into linked list link and link2.

```
// Load objects into a List
loadListObject (link, colors);
// Load integers into a List
loadListInt (link2, num);
```

4. Concatenate the list link with the list link2 and print the concatenated list link.

```
// Concatenate two list
conCat (link, link2);
printList (link);
```

5. Search for an object yell in the linked list link. Output the results of the search.

```
// Locate an object in the list
j = locate (link, yell);
System.out.println ("The location of "+yell+" is = "+j);
```

6. Insert an object in the linked list link before the object tell. Print the list objects.

```
// Insert an object in the list before the object located
insertKey (link, tell, j);
printList (link);
```

7. Locate an object tell in a linked list link. Remove the object tells located in the linked list link and print the linked list link.

```
// Locate an object in the list
j = locate (link, tell);
System.out.println ("The location of"+tell+ "is ="+j);
// Remove an object from the list
removeKey (link, j, j+1);
printList (link);
```

8. Add an object to the front of a linked list link. Add an object to the rear of a linked list link. Print the linked list link.

```
// Add an object in the front of the list
addFront (link, tell);
printList (link);
System.out.println ("The object"+tell+
```

```
    "is added to the front of the list");
    // Add an object in the rear of the list
    addRear (link, tell);
    printList (link);
    System.out.println ("The object"+tell+
    "is added to the rear of the list");
  } // End ListTest
  // Retrieve and print the list information content
  public void printList (List listRef)
  {
    System.out.println ("\nList Output:");
    for (int k = 0; k < listRef.size ( ); k++)
      System.out.print(listRef.get (k) + " ");
    System.out.println ( );
  } // End printList
  // Load object data into List from a String colors and an integer array num
  public void loadListObject (LinkedList A, Object B [ ])
  {
    int k;
    for ( k = 0; k < B.length; k++)
    {
      A.add(B [ k ]);
    } //End for loop
  } // End loadListObject
  // Load integer data into List from a String colors and an integer array num
  public void loadListInt (LinkedList A, int B [ ])
  {
    int k;
    for (k = 0; k < B.length; k++)
    {
      // Convert the numbers to objects
      A.add (new Integer (B [ k ]));
    } // End for loop
  } // End loadListInt
  // Locate an object K in list.
  // Return the index of K in the list.
  // If K is not in the list return -1.
  public int locate (List listRef2, Object K)
  {
```

```
  ListIterator listIt = listRef2.listIterator ( );
  int j = 0;
  while (listIt.hasNext ( ))
   {
     Object obj = listIt.next ( ); // Get an item
     if (obj.equals (K))
      return j;
      j = j + 1;
   } // End while
   return -1;
} // End locate
// Remove an object or a set of objects from the list
// start is the first index of the sublist
// end is the lst index of the sublist
public void removeKey (List listRef, int start, int end)
{
  listRef.subList (start, end).clear ( );   // remove items
} // End removeKey
// Add an object K to the front of the list
public void addFront (List listRef, Object K)
{
  listRef.add (K);
} // End addFront
// Add an object K to the rear of the list
public void addRear (List listRef, Object K)
{
  listRef.add (0, K);
} // End addRear
// Insert an object K to the list at position loc the list
public void insertKey (List listRef, Object K, int loc)
{
  listRef.add (loc, K);
} // End insertKey
// Concatenate list link and link2
// Release the resources of link2
public void conCat (LinkedList link, LinkedList link2)
{
  link.addAll (link2); // Concatenate lists
  link2 = null;        // Release resources
```

} // End conCat

// ------
// main
// ------
public static void main (String args [ ])
{
  new ListTest ( );
} //End main
Figure 19. Linked Lists and ListIterators

Selected methods from the application in Figure 19 are detailed in Sections 4.1.4.1 through 4.1.4.7. Figure 20 details List Class methods.

Type	Method	Description
boolean	add (E o)	Appends the specified element to the end of this list (optional operation).
void	add (int index, E element)	Inserts the specified element at the specified position in this list (optional operation).
boolean	addAll (Collection c)	Appends all of the elements in the specified collection to the end this list, in the order that they are returned by the specified collection's iterator (optional operation).
boolean	addAllint (index, Collection c)	Inserts all of the elements in the specified collection into this list at the specified position (optional operation).
void	clear ( )	Removes all of the elements from this list (optional operation).
boolean	contains (Object o)	Returns true if this list contains the specified element.
boolean	containsAll	Returns true if this list contains

	(Collection c)	all of the elements of the specified collection.
boolean	equals (Object o)	Compares the specified object with this list for equality.
	get(int index)	Returns the element at the specified position in this list.
int	hashCode ( )	Returns the hash code value for this list.
int	indexOf (Object o)	Returns the index in this list of the first occurrence of the specified element, or -1 if this list does not contain this element.
boolean	isEmpty ( )	Returns true if this list contains no elements.
Iterator	iterator ( )	Returns an iterator over the elements in this list in proper sequence.
int	lastIndexOf (Object o)	Returns the index in this list of the last occurrence of the specified element, or -1 if this list does not contain this element.
ListIterator	listIterator ( )	Returns a list iterator of the elements in this list (in proper sequence).
ListIterator	listIterator (int index)	Returns a list iterator of the elements in this list (in proper sequence), starting at the specified position in this list.
	remove (int index)	Removes the element at the specified position in this list (optional operation).
boolean	remove (Object o)	Removes the first occurrence in this list of the specified element (optional operation).
boolean	removeAll (Collection c)	Removes from this list all the elements that are contained in the specified collection (optional operation).

boolean	retainAll (Collection c)	Retains only the elements in this list that are contained in the specified collection (optional operation).
set	(int index, E element)	Replaces the element at the specified position in this list with the specified element (optional operation).
int	size ( )	Returns the number of elements in this list.
List	subList (int fromIndex, int toIndex)	Returns a view of the portion of this list between the specified fromIndex, inclusive, and toIndex, exclusive.
Object [ ]	toArray ( )	Returns an array containing all of the elements in this list in proper sequence.
T [ ]	toArray (T [ ] a)	Returns an array containing all of the elements in this list in proper sequence; the runtime type of the returned array is that of the specified array.

Figure 20. List Class Method Summary
Note: This is a modification of selected information from [14].

4.1.4.1. Load Linked Lists Method loadList

Data are stored as objects in Java. Store an undertermined but finite number of objects in a linked list. A List class method add (Object d) is used to implement the storage of the data in a list. The programmer is free of the responsibility of obtaining a new list node, inserting the new data, linking the new node to the existing list, and returning a pointer to the list. A method called loadListObject from Figure 21 details the loading of object data.

```
// Load object data into List A from an array of objects B
public void loadListObject (LinkedList A, Object B [ ])
{
  int k;
```

```
  for (k = 0; k < B.length; k++)
  {
    A.add (B [ k ]);
    } //End for loop
  } // End loadListObject
```
Figure 21. Load Object Data into a List

Data with primitive data types maybe wrapped as objects and stored in linked list. Strings are defined as objects. Primitive data type's int is wrapped as Integer, char is wrapped as Character, and double is wrapped as Double. A method called loadListInt from Figure 22 details the loading of primitive data type data.

```
// Load integer data into List A from an array of integers
public void loadListInt (LinkedList A, int B [ ])
{
  int k;
  for (k = 0; k < B.length; k++)
  {
    // Convert the numbers to objects
    A.add (new Integer (B [ k ]));
    } // End for loop
  } // End loadListInt
```
Figure 23. Load Primitive Datatype int Data into a List

4.1.4.2. Concatenate Linked Lists Method conCat

In order to concatenate two linked list a pointer to the end of the first list must be known. The user must find or design the list with a pointer to the beginning and a pointer to the end of the list. The list concatenation involves inserting the pointer to the second list in the link field of the first list. The pointer to the beginning of the first list is returned as the pointer to the concatenated list. A List class method from Figure 20 called addAll performs list concatenation. The user is freed from the details of list concatenations. This reduces implementation errors and minimizes the time to fast prototype an application. List concatenation is detailed in the method called conCat from Figure 24 using the List class method addAll from Figure 20.

```
// Concatenate list link and link2
// Release the resources of link2
public void conCat (LinkedList link, LinkedList link2)
```

```
{
  link.addAll (link2);  // Concatenate lists
  link2 = null;          // Release resources
} // End conCat
```
Figure 24. Concatenate Linked Lists

4.1.4.3. Search for a Key in a Linked Lists Method locate

Find a key K in the list. This list operation requires operations to compare the content of a list node with the search key, if there is a match stop and reply a successful search, if there is no match move to the next node and continue the search by comparing the node content to the search key until the end of the list, and at the end of the list stop and reply unsuccessful search. These steps require programming several methods. This increases implementation time and the programming process may increase programming errors. The List class offers several methods to implement a list search for a key. The List class methods are detailed in Figure 20. Searches of a linked list for a key is detailed in a method called locate in Figure 25.

```
// Locate an object K in list.
// Return the index of K in the list.
// If K is not in the list return -1.
public int locate (List listRef2, Object K)
{
  ListIterator listIt = listRef2.listIterator ( );
  int j = 0;
  while (listIt.hasNext ( ))
  {
    Object obj = listIt.next ( ); // Get an item
    if (obj.equals (K))
    return j;
    j = j + 1;
  } // End while
  return -1;
} // End locate
```
Figure 25. Locate an Object K in a Linked List

4.1.4.4. Insert a key in a Linked Lists Method insertKey

A key may be inserted in a linked list at any location pointed to by a list pointer. In a single linked list the user must program to provide a trailing pointer that points to the node that contain the pointer to the node that the user plan to insert the new node before it. The trailing pointer must be maintained under programmer control by the user. The insertion involves inserting the pointer of the node that follows the new node in the link field of the new node, which is the pointer in the node pointed to by the trailing pointer, and insert the pointer to the new node in the link field of the node pointed to by the trailing pointer. A new node is inserted in a list before a node pointed to by loc using a method from the List class called add (pointer, Object) detailed in Figure 20. All these operations are accomplished with one method call. Errors are reduced since one programming step replaces several steps that requires the user to program the basic steps required to insert a node in an existing list before any node pointed to by loc. Figure 26 details a method to insert a node in a list before a node pointed to by loc.

```
// Insert an object K into the list at position loc in the list
public void insertKey (List listRef, Object K, int loc)
{
  listRef.add (loc, K);
} // End insertKey
```
Figure 26. Insert an Object K into the List at Position Loc in the List

4.1.4.5. Remove a Key From a Linked Lists Method removeKey

Removing a node from a single linked list is as complicated as inserting a node in a list. A trailing pointer must be available. A trailing pointer is detailed in Section 4.1.4.4. The node pointed to by the trailing pointer link field is set to the content of the node link field that is removed. The node is returned to the available storage pool. Several methods and detail knowledge about list processing programming is required to implement a list node removal. A list node is removed using two methods called subList (int start, int end) and clear ( ) from the List class detailed in Figure 20. Figure 27 details a method to remove a node from a list using subList (int start, int end) and clear ( ).

```
// Remove an object or a set of objects from a list
// start is the first index of the sublist
// end is the last index of the sublist
public void removeKey (List listRef, int start, int end)
{
```

listRef.subList (start, end).clear ( ); // remove items
} // End removeKey
Figure 27. Remove an Object or a Set of Objects from a List

4.1.4.6. Add a Key to the Front of a Linked Lists Method addFront

A new node is added to an existing list in a few steps if a pointer to the end of the list is known. If a pointer to the end of a single linked list is not known the user must traverse the list using a trailing pointer to locate the end of the list. A list node must be allocated. The node link field on the existing list pointed to by the trailing pointer is set to the pointer to the new allocated node. A pointer to the end of the list is set to the pointer to the new node. Implementing these steps require detail list processing knowledge and the programming may produce errors. Adding a new node to the front of a list requires one method called add (Object) detailed in the List class in Figure 20. Figure 28 details a method to add a node to the front of an existing list.

```
// Add an object K to the front of a list
public void addFront (List listRef, Object K)
{
  listRef.add (K);
} // End addFront
```
Figure 28. Add an Object K to the Front of a List

4.1.4.7. Add a Key to the Rear of a Linked Lists Method addRear

A new node is added to an existing list in two steps in a single linked list. Most lists are designed to have a pointer to the rear or first node in the list. A list node must be allocated. The link field of the new node is set to the pointer to the rear of the existing list. The pointer to the rear of the link is set to the pointer to the new list node. Implementing these steps require detail list processing knowledge and the programming may produce errors. Adding a new node to the rear of a list requires one method called add (loc, Object) detailed in the List class in Figure 20. Figure 29 details a method to add a node to the rear of an existing list.

```
// Add an object K to the rear of a list
public void addRear (List listRef, Object K)
{
  listRef.add (0, K);
} // End addRear
```
Figure 29. Add an Object K to the Rear of a List

4.2. Load Data Into a HashSet

This class implements the Set interface, backed by a hash table. The iteration order may vary and the iteration time may not be constant over time. This class permits the null element.

Constant performance time for basic operations methods add, remove, contains, and size achieved when the hash function disperses the elements properly among the buckets. Iterating over this set requires time proportional to the sum of the HashSet number of elements plus the number of buckets. A moderate capacity yields a moderate load factor which yields an optimum iteration performance.

The HashSet class is a concrete class that implements Set. It can be used to store duplicate-free elements. Objects added to a hash set need to implement the hashCode method in a manner that properly disperses the hash code. A hash set is created that reads data from an input device, and uses an iterator to traverse the elements in the set is detailed in Figure 30. A selected class HashSet application is detailed with a range of steps:

1. Start a class setHash with methods Ibuf, Inf, readDouble, and selected methods from the HashSet class to store student grades.

```
import java.util.*;
import javax.swing.*;
import java.io.*;
public class setHash
{
    //------------------------------------------------------
    // Setup File Reference Handle for File Name
    //------------------------------------------------------
    public static BufferedReader Ibuf (String filename)
    throws java.io.IOException
    {
      // Setup the basic input stream
      FileReader fr = new FileReader (filename);
      // Buffer the input stream
      BufferedReader br = new BufferedReader (fr);
      return br;
    } // End Ibuf
    //----------------------
```

```
// Input a Data Item
//---------------------
public static String Inf (BufferedReader br)
throws java.io.IOException
{ String inval;
   if ((inval = br.readLine ( )) != null)
   {
      return inval;
   } else return null;
} // End Inf
// ------------------------------------------------
// Read a double value from the input device
// ------------------------------------------------
public static double readDouble (BufferedReader HL)
throws java.io.IOException
{ String tval;
   tval = Inf (HL);
   if (tval == null) return -1.00;
   else return Double.parseDouble (tval);
} // End readDouble
// ----------------
// main method
// --------------
public static void main (String [ ] args)
throws java.io.IOException
{
```

2. Allocate a HashSet container tableHash using a HashSet constructor.
   // Create a hash set from data on an input device
   Set tableHash = new HashSet ( );
   String Fname = " "; // Input file name
   // Input the grade file path and name

3. Receive a path and file name of student grades using an input dialog box. Read the data with BufferedReader input. Store the objects in a HashSet table-Hash with an add method from the HashSet class.
   Fname = JOptionPane.showInputDialog ("Enter the Path"+
   "and FileName");
   BufferedReader HT = Ibuf (Fname);

```
// Read scores and find the best score
// An empty input device file terminates input
do
  {
    // Read a score from the input device
    double score = readDouble (HT);
    // End of file on negative score
    if (score < 0) break;
    tableHash.add (new Double (score));
  } while (true);
```

4. Display the number of students added to the HashSet and prints the table-Hash using an iterator.

```
// Display the number of students
JOptionPane.showMessageDialog (null, "Total Number of"+
    "Students "+tableHash.size ( ));
// Output the data in the hashSet
System.out.println (tableHash);
// Obtain an iterator for the hashSet
Iterator iterator = tableHash.iterator ( );
// Display the elements in the hash set
while (iterator.hasNext ( ))
  {
    System.out.print (iterator.next ( ) + " ");
  } // End while
```

5. Create a sorted tree set from the HashSet tableHash. Print the sorted tree set of strings.

```
// Create a sorted tree set from the hash set for strings
Set treeSet = new TreeSet (tableHash);
System.out.println ("\n\nA sorted tree set of strings");
System.out.println (treeSet + "\n");
  } // End main
} // End class setHash
```
Figure 30. Load the Student Grades into a Hashset

4.3. SortedSets and TreeSets
A TreeSet is based on red-black trees. These trees are something like binary trees, with a collection of nodes containing left and right subtrees. However the trees

have additional functionality to keep them balanced, that is, to keep their shape from becoming skewed and thereby degrading tree lookup performance. A review of selected Trees is included since TreeSet involves trees.

4.3.1. General Trees

A general tree T is a finite set of one or more nodes such that there is one designated node r, called the root of T, and the remaining nodes are partitioned into n = 0 disjoint subsets T_1, T_2, ..., T_n, each of which is a tree, and whose roots r_1, r_2, ..., r_n, respectively, are children of r. A general tree is detailed in Figure 31.

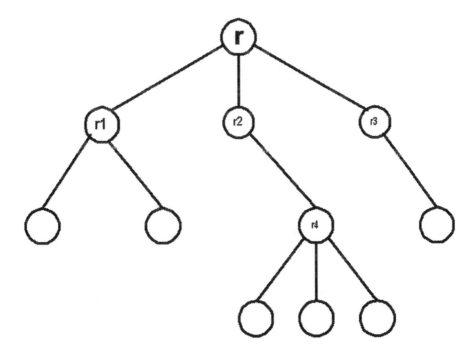

Figure 31. General Tree

It follows from our definition that every node of a tree is the root of some subtree contained in the whole tree. The number of subtrees of a node is called the degree of the node. A node of degree zero is called a terminal node or sometimes a "leaf." A non-terminal node is often called a branch node. The level of a node with respect to T is defined by saying that the root has level 0, and other nodes have a level that is one higher than they have with respect to the subtree of the root, T_j which contains them.

The root in Figure 31 is r, and its three subtrees {r1}, {r2, r4}, and {r3}. The tree {r2} has node r as its root. Node r2 is on level 1 with respect to the whole tree, and it has one subtree {r4}. Therefore f2 has degree 1.

Standard terminology for tree structures is taken from the second form of family tree, the lineal chart: Each root is said to be the father of the roots of its subtree, and the latter are said to be brothers, and they are sons of their father. The root of the entire tree has no father. For example, in Figure 31, r4 has three sons.

4.3.2. Binary Trees

A binary tree is a finite set of elements that is either empty or contains a single element called the root of the tree and whose remaining elements are partitioned into disjoint subsets, each of which is itself a binary tree. These two subsets are called the left and right subtrees of the original tree. Each element of a binary tree is called a node of the tree. A binary tree is detailed in Figure 32.

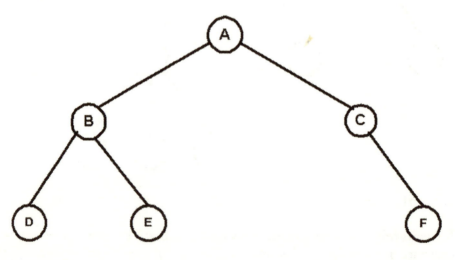

Figure 32. Binary Tree

The tree in Figure 32 consists of six nodes with A as its root. Its left subtree is rooted at B and its right subtree is rooted at C. This is indicated by the two branches emanating from A: to B on the left and to C on the right. The absence of a branch indicates an empty subtree. The binary trees rooted at D, E, and F has empty right and left subtrees.

If n1 is the root of a binary tree and n2 is the root of its left or right subtree, then n1 is said to be the father of n2 and n2 is said to be the left or right son of n1. A node that has no sons is called a leaf node. Node n1 is an ancestor of node n2 if n1 is either the father of n2 or the father of some ancestor of n2. A node n2 is a left descendant of node n1 if n2 is either the left son of n1 or a descendant of the left son of n1. A right descendant may be similarly defined. Two nodes are brothers if they are left and right sons of the same father.

The root of the tree has level 0 and the level of any other node in the tree is one more than the level of its father. For example, the binary tree of Figure 32, node B is at level 1 and F is at level 2. A complete binary tree of level n is one in which each node of level n is a leaf and in which each node of level less than n has nonempty left and right subtrees.

A linked binary tree pointed to by a link variable IT is detailed in Figure 33.

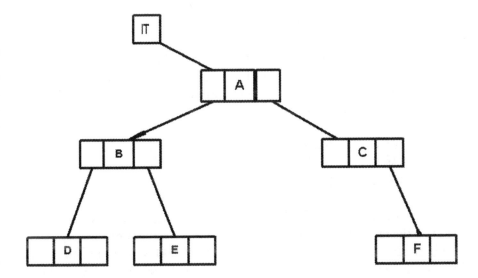

Figure 33. Linked Binary Tree

Binary Tree Traversals

One of the most common operations performed on tree structures is that of traversal. This is a procedure by which each node is processed exactly once in some systematic manner. This terminology was popularized by Knuth [3]. We can traverse a binary tree in three ways namely, in preorder, in inorder, and in postorder. These traversals are defined with recursive definitions.

> Preorder traversal
>> Process the root.
>> Traverse the left subtree in preorder.
>> Traverse the right subtree in preorder.

> Inorder traversal
>> Traverse the left subtree in inorder.
>> Process the root node
>> Traverse the right subtree in inorder.
> Postorder traversal
>> Traverse the left subtree in postorder
>> Traverse the right subtree in postorder.
>> Process the root node.

If a particular subtree is empty, the traversal is performed by doing nothing. In other words, a null subtree is considered to be fully traversed when it is encountered. The preorder, inorder, and postorder traversals of the binary tree in Figure 33 will process the nodes in the following order:

> ABDECF   (preorder)
> DBEACF   (inorder)
> DEBFCA   (postorder)

These binary tree traversal definitions are implemented as non-recursive algorithms to improve the reader's knowledge in list processing. Programming these algorithms will enhance the readers programming skills by operating close to the LISP paradigm. Algorithm F implements a binary tree preorder traversal in [9]. Algorithm H implements a binary tree inorder traversal in [9]. Algorithm G implements a binary tree postorder traversal in [9].

4.3.3. Binary Search Trees

A binary search tree t is a binary tree; either it is empty or each node in the tree contains an identifier and:

(i) all identifiers in the left subtree of t are less (numerically or alphabetically) than the identifier in the root node t;

(ii) all identifiers in the right subtree of t are greater than the identifier in the rootnode of t;

(iii) the left and right subtrees of t are also binary search trees.

For a given set of identifiers several binary search trees are possible. To determine whether an identifier x is present in a binary search tree, x is compared with the root. If a is less than the identifier in the root, then the search continues in the left subtree; if x equals the identifier in the root, the search terminates successfully; otherwise the search continues in the right subtree. This is formalized in algorithm S. A binary search tree is detailed in Figure 34.

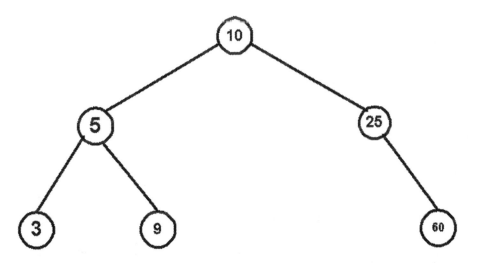

Figure 34. Binary Search Tree

In evaluating binary search trees, it is useful to add a null in the link fields of the terminal nodes. Every binary tree with n nodes has n + 1 null links. Nodes with null links are called external nodes. The nodes without null links are internal nodes. Each time a binary search tree is examined for an identifier which is not in the tree, the search terminates at an external or failure node. We define the external path length of a binary tree to be the sum over all external nodes of the lengths of the paths from the root to those nodes. An internal path length is defined to be the sum over all internal nodes of the lengths of the paths from the root to those nodes. For the tree of Figure 34 we obtain its internal path length, K, to be:

$$K = 0 + 2 + 1 + 2 = 5$$

Its external path length, E, is:

$$E = 3 + 2 + 3 = 8.$$

The internal and external path lengths of a binary tree with n internal nodes are related by the formula E = K + 2n. The worst case occurs when the tree is skewed. The value of K for a skewed tree is,

$$K = \sum_{i=0}^{n-1} i = n(n-1)/2.$$

The trees with minimal K must have as many internal nodes as close to the root as possible. The smallest value for K is

$$\sum_{i \leq j \leq n} \log_2 j = O(n \log_2 n).$$

Information on binary search trees are detailed in [9].

4.4. Class TreeSet

A set is a collection of elements without any duplicates. The Set and SortedSet interfaces describe the properties of sets, and the HashSet, LinkedHashSet, and TreeSet classes implement these interfaces. A typical output from a HashSet, LinkedHashSet, and TreeSet of the same data is detailed in Figure 35. A HashSet, LinkedHashSet, and TreeSet program with random input data is detailed with a range of steps:

1. Define the class SetTest.

```
// -------------------------------------------------------
// HashSet, LinkHashSet, and TreeSet of Data
// -------------------------------------------------------
```

```
import java.util.*;
public class SetTest
{
static final int MIN = 1;
static final int MAX = 10;
// ----------------
// main method
// ----------------
public static void main (String args [ ])
{
 int inp [ ] = new int [12];
 int i;
```

2. Generate uniform random integers for input.

```
// Generate random integer input
System.out.print ("Random Numbers Generated = [");
for (i = 0; i <= 10; ++i)
{ inp [ i ] = 1 + (int)(Math.random ( ) * 50);
   if (i < 10) System.out.print (inp [ i ]+ ",");
   else System.out.println (inp [ i ]+" ]");
} // End for
// Allocate a HashSet container
Set sethash = new HashSet ( );
```

3. Add the random objects to the HashSet.

```
for (i = MAX; i >= MIN; i--)
{ // Add an object to the HashSet
  sethash.add (new Integer (inp [ i ]));
} // End for
System.out.println ("HashSet =" + sethash);
// Allocate a LinkedHashSet container
Set setlink = new LinkedHashSet ( );
```

4. Add the random objects to the LinkedHashSet.

```
for (i = MAX; i >= MIN; i--)
{ // Add an object to the LinkedHashSet
  setlink.add (new Integer (inp [ i ]));
} // End for
System.out.println ("LinkedHashSet =" + setlink);
```

```
// Allocate a TreeSet container
Set settree = new TreeSet ( );
```

5. Add the random objects to the TreeSet
```
for (i = MAX; i >= MIN; i--)
{ // Add an object to the TreeSet
  settree.add (new Integer (inp [ i ]));
} // End for
System.out.println ("TreeSet =" + settree);
} // End main
} // End class SetTest
```
6. Printed output of the HashSet, LinkedHashSet, and TreeSet objects.
Random Numbers Generated = [22, 35, 18, 20, 44, 41, 18, 47, 50, 28, 42]
HashSet = [47, 41, 28, 50, 18, 20, 35, 42, 22, 44]
LinkedHashSet = [42, 28, 50, 47, 18, 41, 44, 20, 35, 22]
TreeSet = [18, 20, 22, 28, 35, 41, 42, 44, 47, 50]
Figure 35. Output from HashSet, LinkedHashSet, and TreeSet of the Same Input

Elements in a HashSet are retrieved with iteration ordering. The elements of a LinkedHashSet are retrieved in the order that they are inserted into the set. Elements of a TreeSet are retrieved in ascending sorted order.

A HashSet is for representing sets if element ordering is not important. But if ordering is important, then LinkedHashSet or TreeSet are better. However, LinkedHashSet or TreeSet come with an additional speed and space cost.

A TreeSet can be generated from a HashSet. The program segment in Figure 38 generates a TreeSet from a HashTable detailed in Figure 5. This program segment is included in the HashSet application in Figure 30. TreeSet class constructors are detailed in Figure 36. Other TreeSet class methods are detailed in Figure 37.

Method	Description
TreeSet ( )	Construct a new TreeSet whose backing TreeMap using the "natural" ordering of keys.
TreeSet (Collection collection)	Construct a new TreeSet whose backing TreeMap uses the "natural" orering of

		the keys and which contains all of the elements in the supplied Collection.
TreeSet (Comparator comparator)		Construct a new TreeSet whose backing TreeMap uses the supplied Comparator.
private TreeSet (SortedMap backingMap)		This private constructor is used to implement the subSet( ) calls around a backing TreeMap.
SubMap	TreeSet (SortedSet sortedSet)	Construct a new TreeSet, using the same keyordering as the supplied SortedSet and containing all of the elements in the supplied SortedSet.

Figure 36. TreeSet Constructor Summary
Note: This is a modification of selected information from [14].

Type	Method	Description
boolean	add (java.lang. Object obj)	Adds the supplied Object to the Set if it is not already in the Set; returns true if the element is added, false otherwise.
boolean	addAll (Collection c)	Adds all of the elements in the upplied Collection to this TreeSet.
void	clear ( )	Removes all elements in this Set. java.lang.
Object	clone ( )	Returns a shallow copy of this Set.
Comparator	comparator ( )	Returns this Set's comparator.
boolean	contains (java.lang.Object obj)	Returns true if this Set contains the supplied Object, false otherwise.
java.lang. Object	first ( )	Returns the first (by order) element in this Set.
SortedSet	headset (java.lang.Object to)	Returns a view of this Set including all elements less than to.

boolean	isEmpty ( )	Returns true if this Set has size 0, false otherwise.
Iterator	iterator ( )	Returns in Iterator over the elements in this TreeSet, which traverses in ascending order.
java.lang. Object	last ( )	Returns the last (by order) element in this Set.
private void	readObject (java.io.Object In put Streams)	Deserializes this object from the given stream.
boolean	remove (java.lang.Object obj)	If the supplied Object is in this Set, it is removed, and true is returned; otherwise, false is returned.
int	size ( )	Returns the number of elements in this Set
SortedSet	subSet (java.lang.Object from, java.lang.Object to)	Returns a view of this Set including all elements greater or equal to from and less than to (a half-open interval).
SortedSet	tailSet (java.lang.Object from)	Returns a view of this Set including all elements greater or equal to from.
private void	writeObject (java.io.Object OutputStreams)	Serializes this object to the given stream.

Figure 37. TreeSet Method Summary
Note: This is a modification of selected information from [14].

```
// Create a sorted tree set from the hash set for strings
Set treeSet = new TreeSet (tableHash);
System.out.println ("\n\nA sorted tree set of strings");
System.out.println (treeSet + "\n");
```
Figure 38. Create a Sorted Tree Set From a Hash Set of Strings

4.5. Exercises

1. Implement an algorithm as a method or set of methods to setup a linked queue with a front pointer F and a back pointer B. Implement a method to invoke the PoP method for the queue and display each data item in a GUI interface message box. Terminate the display when the queue is empty. Load the arrival time from a hard disk file called CAR.DAT into the queue. The data stored as one number per record in CAR.DAT are 2, 8, 20, 10, 6, 12, 50, 4, 1, and 30. CAR.DAT has 10 data items; however, the input must be designed for an unknown number of items. Assign a positive integer name to each arrival drawn from a uniform random distribution.

2. Load the data in problem 1 into the linked queue. Use the linked queue from problem 1 pointed to by F and B to implement an algorithm as methods to implement a server with time slices drawn from a uniform random distribution. On each simulation cycle the server pops the queue, decrements the car arrival time (New Arrival Time = Current Car Arrival Time—Server Time Slice), if a car new arrival time is zero or less delete the car from the queue, else if the car new arrival time is greater than zero push the car new arrival time with its attributes on the queue. Count the number of simulation cycles per car, number of cars in the queue, and the total number of simulation cycles. At each cycle of the simulation the car name, current arrival time, server time slice, simulation cycles per car, and cumulative simulation cycles are displayed in a GUI dialog box. The algorithm terminates when the queue is empty.

Implement an algorithm as a method or set of methods to setup a linked stack pointed to by a linked variable B. Load the information from a hard disk file called STK.DAT into the stack. The data stored as one number per record in STK.DAT are 2, 260, 7, 4, 7, 3, 450, 700, 3, 88, 600, 6, 300, 100, 3, 6, 80, 50, and 10. The number 3 is +; 4 is -; 6 is *; 7 is /, and 2 is =. STK.DAT has 19 data items; however, the input must be designed for an unknown number of items. Display the data in the linked stack pointed to by B. The data are to be displayed in a graphics user interface (GUI) message box.

Note on triples:
Method to generate triples from the data in the input stack. Setup an array TMP of temporaries T1, T2, .., T10. Implement a Triple Algorithm.

Algorithm G. Triple Generator

G1. [Initialize] i = -1; IP points to the input Stack. IQ points to the output stack.

G2. [Pop the input stack] while (IP != 0) {   KP = Pop (IP);

G3. [Is this an Operator?] if (KP == Operator)
{ OP1 = Pop (IQ); IP2 = Pop (IQ);
//Generate a Triple
Trip [i+1][0] = KP; Trip [i+1][1] = OP1; Trip [i+1][2] = OP2;
//Push the temporary onto the output stack
i= i+1; Push (IQ, TMP [i]); } // End Operator

G4. [It is not an operator.] Push (IQ, KP);
} //End while on Input Stack

G5. [Output all Triples] for (j = 0; j <=i; ++j) print (Trip[j][0], Trip[j][1], Trip[j][2]);

4. Load the stack with the data and setup code from problem 3. Design and implement algorithms as methods to generate triples from the information in the stack. Post all the output in one GUI dialog box.

5. Implement an algorithm as a method or set of methods to setup a linked list to simulate task in an operating system. Load the task arrival times from a hard disk file called TASK.DAT into the list with priorities assigned to each arrival from a uniform random distribution. Example int prority = (int)(1 + (Math.random ( ) *5)). Assign a positive integer name to each task. The arrival time data stored as one number per record in TASK.DAT are 2, 8, 20, 10, 6, 12, 50, 4, 1, and 30. TASK.DAT has 10 data items; however, the input must be designed for an unknown number of items. Hint: use a while statement and the fact that Java read a null as the end of file with BufferedReader input. Display the data in the linked list. The data are to be displayed in a graphics user interface (GUI) message box are task arrival times, task priority, and task name.

6. Use the linked list from problem 5, and implement an algorithm as methods to implement a server with time slices and priorities drawn from uniform random distributions. The server serves one task in each pass through the linked list. A pass is defined as a cycle through the linked list to find a task with a priority nearest the one drawn from the uniform distribution by the server. The server decrements a Task arrival time by the time slice drawn form a uniform distribution by the server with the nearest priority on each simulation cycle. Difference = Current Task Arrival Time—Current Server Time Slice. At each cycle of the simulation the task name,

time, priority, server time slice, and server priority are printed in a GUI dialog box. If the server Difference is zero or less delete the Task from the list. Otherwise, the Task new arrival time Difference and the current server priority time are used to update the current Task list node. The algorithm terminates when the list is empty.

7. Insert code in the ListTest class in Figure 19 that implements the clear, contains, equal, hashCode, indexOf, isEmpty, LastIndexOf, listIterator, remove, set, and toArray methods described in Figure 20.

8. Insert code in the setHash class in Figure 30 that implements the clear, headset, isEmpty, last, remove, and tailset methods described in Figure 36 and Figure 37.

5. Implementing an e-Business Application

The server systems administrator can execute a PHP command on the server to hide all PHP code from view in a client machine browser. To avoid user viewing the PDCRS web page codes on the server most of the PDCRS web pages are embedded in PHP.

5.1. Performance Data Collection and Reporting

Collect performance data from components of an organization. Allow the users to register a profile. Data are collected on best practices and organization statistics. Results are generated by the user from a list of aggregates from user data. A registered user should be able to change their data at any time. The application must use relational database technologies to store and retrieve user data. Data are received from users with client machines executing a browser connected to a web server.

5.2. User Registration and Login to the Performance Data Collection Report System (PDCRS)

Data are collected from the user to define a user profile. The users are registered and account information posted to the user. Registered users are allowed to change their profile data at any time with their identification and password code. Users are not allowed to change their user account number that was assigned by the performance data collection and reporting system (PDCRS).

5.3. Registration of Users

User registration data are stored in a PDCRS database table called users. A Structured Query Language (SQL) command that created the PDCRS users table is detailed in Figure 39.

CREATE TABLE users (ID MEDIUMINT NOT NULL AUTO_INCREMENT PRIMARY KEY,
 username VARCHAR(60), password VARCHAR(60))
Figure 39. Create a PDCRS User Data Table

5.3.1. Registration and Login Form Fields

Registration data are user identification, password, and a verification password. A form in Figure 40 details the form fields for registration.

```
<form action="<?php echo $_SERVER['PHP_SELF']; ?>" method="post">
<table border="0">
<tr><td>Username:</td><td>
<input type="text" name="username" maxlength="60">
</td></tr>
<tr><td>Password:</td><td>
<input type="password" name="pass" maxlength="10">
</td></tr>
<tr><td>Confirm Password:</td><td>
<input type="password" name="pass2" maxlength="10">
</td></tr>
<tr><th colspan=2><input type="submit" name="submit" value="Register"></th></tr>
</table>
</form>
```
Figure 40. Registration Form Fields

Login form field data are user identification and password. Login form fields are detailed in Figure 41.

```
<form action="actlog.php" method="post">
<table border="0">
<tr><td colspan=2><h1>Login</h1></td></tr>
<tr><td>Username:</td><td>
<input type="text" name="username" maxlength="40">
</td></tr>
<tr><td>Password:</td><td>
<input type="password" name="pass" maxlength="50">
</td></tr
```

```
<tr><td colspan="2" align="right">
<input type="submit" name="submit" value="Login">
</td></tr>
</table>
</form>
```
Figure 41. Login Form Fields

5.3.2. Register a User Script

PDCRS users are registered automatically using a registration script. The registration script sets the web page color, connects the user to the PDCRS database, and request user identification and password. User identification and password data are verified for completeness. Incomplete user input generates a message to the user and the user is instructed to try a new registration. Verified user identification and password data are checked against the users table to insure that user identifications are unique. The cleared user identification is stored with its associated password in the users table. An account number is assigned to the user and a blank record is written to the user profile table and the performance data table pdata. A successful user registration message is posted to the user. The PDCRS registration script is detailed with a range of steps:

1. Set the script to be executed on the server. Start a web page embedded in PHP.
```
<?php
// -------------------------------------------------------------------------------------
// Register users in the performance data collection and reporting system (PDCRS)
// -------------------------------------------------------------------------------------
echo '<html>';
echo '<body  BGCOLOR=#D66321>';
```

2. Connect to the database on the MySQL relational database server. Set the database to pdcrs.
```
// Connect to the PDCRS Database
mysql_connect('localhost', 'pdcrs', '  ') or die(mysql_error( ));
mysql_select_db('pdcrs') or die(mysql_error( ));
```
3. Check for a form in which the user pressed the form submit key. If no submit key was pressed the script posted the form for user input in step 7.
```
// Was the user registration form submitted?
if (isset($_POST['submit']))
```

{
4. The registration form submits key has been pressed. The registration form fields are username or user identification, pass or password, and pass2 or password verification. Check for filled fields in the form. Post a user message to the user for incomplete data and instruct the user to perform a new registration completing all form fields.

```
// Check the form for blank fields
if (!$_POST['username'] | !$_POST['pass'] | !$_POST['pass2'])
{
   die('<p>You did not complete all of the required fields</p><a href =
   "index.html">Click Here to Register</a>');
} // End if blank field
```

5. Correct form fields are checked against the users table for unique username or identification. A duplicate username triggers a user message to the user that the username existed. The user is instructed to perform a new registration with a new username. The registration two password fields are checked. If the registration forms two passwords are not the same a message is posted to the user about the incorrect passwords and the user is instructed to try a new registration with correct data.

```
// Checks for duplicate usernames
if (!get_magic_quotes_gpc( ))
{
   $_POST['username'] = addslashes($_POST['username']);
} // End if duplicate username
// Get the username from the users table
$usercheck = $_POST['username'];
$check = mysql_query("SELECT username FROM users WHERE username =
'$usercheck'")
or die(mysql_error( ));
$check2 = mysql_num_rows($check);
// If the name exists exit to avoid duplicate names
if ($check2 != 0)
{
   die('<p>Sorry, the username '.$_POST['username'].' is already in use.</p>'.
   '<a href = "index.html">Click Hear to Register</a>');
} // End if duplicate found
// Verify that the two passwords are the same
if ($_POST['pass'] != $_POST['pass2'])
```

```
{
  die('<p>Your passwords did not match.</p> <a href="index.html">Click Here to
  Register</a> ');
} // End if password
// Encrypt the password and add slashes if needed
$_POST['pass'] = md5($_POST['pass']);
if (!get_magic_quotes_gpc( ))
{
  $_POST['pass'] = addslashes($_POST['pass']);
  $_POST['username'] = addslashes($_POST['username']);
} // End if
```

6. The username and password are valid. Insert the username and password into the users table in the database. A user account number is assigned automatically using an automatically incremented users table primary key ID. Insert a blank record with a primary key ID in the profile table for user profile data and the pdata table for performance data. Switch to the client machine and post a successful registration message to the user.

```
// The username and password are valid. Insert the username and password into the
// database
$insert = "INSERT INTO users (username, password) VALUES
("".$_POST['username']."", "".$_POST['pass'].""")";
$add_member = mysql_query($insert);
// Insert a profile record for this user into the dstsbase
$insert = "INSERT INTO profile (fname, lname, address, city, state, zipcode,
phone, email) VALUES (' ', ' ', ' ', ' ', ' ', ' ', ' ', ' ')";
$add_member = mysql_query($insert);
$z1 = 0;
// Insert a pdata record for this user into the performance data table
  $insert = "INSERT INTO pdata (orgname, bestpra, numprod, prodsale,
numemp)
VALUES (' ', ' ', '$z1','$z1','$z1')";
$add_member = mysql_query($insert);
?>
  <!-- Report a successful registration to the user -->
  <h1>Registered</h1>
  <p>Thank you, you have registered.</p>
  <!-- Return to Main Menu to Login -->
  <a href= "index.html">Click Here to Login</a>
```

```
<?php
} // End if isset
else
{
 ?>
```

7. The script is set to execute the registration form on the user client machine until the submit button is pressed. When the form submits button is pressed a form action script is executed to extract the form input fields. The registration form action script is set to execute on the server. After the registration form submits button is pressed the server script is executed that includes step 3.

```
<!-- The PDCRS registration form -->
<form action="<?php echo $_SERVER['PHP_SELF']; ?>" method="post">
<table border="0">
<tr><td>Username:</td><td>
<input type="text" name="username" maxlength="60">
</td></tr>
<tr><td>Password:</td><td>
<input type="password" name="pass" maxlength="10">
</td></tr>
<tr><td>Confirm Password:</td><td>
<input type="password" name="pass2" maxlength="10">
</td></tr>
 <tr><th colspan=2><input type="submit" name="submit" value="Register"></th></tr>
 </table>
 </form>
 <?php
} // End ifelse isset
echo '</body>';
echo '</html>';
?>
```

5.3.3. Login a User Script

The PDCRS web pages are stored on the server. Users execute the PDCRS web page from their client machine through their web browser. Registered users login by clicking the login button that executes a PDCRS login script on the server. A login form is posted to the user for input of user identification or username and a password. Start a login web page, set the browser to execute the login form on the client machine followed by setting the web page color. Complete the form fields and press the submit button labeled Login to execute the login form action script.

```
<?php
// ----------------------------------------------------------------------------------------
// Logon Users to the performance data collection and reports system (PDCRS)
// ----------------------------------------------------------------------------------------
?>
<html>
<body  BGCOLOR=#D66321>
<form action="actlog.php" method="post">
<table border="0">
<tr><td colspan=2><h1>Login</h1></td></tr>
<tr><td>Username:</td><td>
<input type="text" name="username" maxlength="40">
</td></tr>
<tr><td>Password:</td><td>
<input type="password" name="pass" maxlength="50">
</td></tr
<tr><td colspan="2" align="right">
<input type="submit" name="submit" value="Login">
</td></tr>
</table>
</form>
</body>
</html>
```

5.3.3.1. Login Form Action Script

A login form action script is executed to extract the user input. The input is verified against the user information stored in the users table. An invalid username causes an error message to be posted to the user with a request for the user to register in the PDCRS. A correct match of the form username and the users table username clears the user as a valid user. The account number for a valid user is written in a temporary file called p.tmp on the client computer. The user account number is used to access all user data in the PDCRS. A menu of options is posted to the valid user for actions in the PDCRS. The PDCRS login script form action script is detailed with a range of steps:

1. Start a web page and set the page color.

```
<!-- ------------------------------------------------------------------------ --
>
<!-- Logon Users to the performance data collection and reports system (PDCRS)
-->
<!-- ------------------------------------------------------------------------ --
>
<html>
<!-- Set the HTML page color -->
<body  BGCOLOR=#D66321>
```

2. Set the browser to receive HTML code from the server. Connect the user to the MySQL server and open the PDCRS database pdcrs.

```
<?php
// Connect to the PDCRS database
mysql_connect('localhost', 'pdcrs', '  ') or die(mysql_error( ));
mysql_select_db('pdcrs') or die(mysql_error( ));
```

3. The login form fields are username or user identification and pass or password. Check for filled fields in the form. Post a user message to the user for incomplete data and instruct the user to perform a new login completing all form fields.

```
// Are the login form fields filled?
if (!$_POST['username'] | !$_POST['pass'])
  {
    die('<p>You did not fill in a required field.<a href = "index.html">Click Here to
    Login</a>');
  }
```

4. A correct username form field is checked against the users table for a username or identification match. A matched username in the users table clears the user as valid. The password for the valid user is checked. If the username and password are valid step 5 is executed. If the login form username does not match a users table username a message is posted to the user about the incorrect information and the user is instructed to try a new login with correct data or the user is instructed to perform a new user registration.

```
// Check the form fields against the users table
// Get the users record set
```

```
$check = mysql_query("SELECT id, username, password FROM users WHERE
username = '".$_POST['username'].'"')or die(mysql_error( ));
// Check for a valid user
$check2 = mysql_num_rows($check);
if ($check2 == 0)
  {
   die('<p>That user does not exist in the PDCRS users table. <a
   href="reguser.php">Click Here to Register</a></p>');
  }
// Check the user password
while($info = mysql_fetch_array ($check))
  {
   $_POST['pass'] = stripslashes($_POST['pass']);
   $info['password'] = stripslashes($info['password']);
   $_POST['pass'] = md5($_POST['pass']);
   // Check for an invalid password
   if ($_POST['pass'] != $info['password'])
   {
     die('<p>Incorrect password, please try again.</p><a href = "index.html">Click
     Here to Login</a>');
   }
   else
   {
```

5. Query the users table and generate a record set for the valid user and retrieve the user account number ID.

```
   // Get the user record set for the account from the users table
   $check = mysql_query("SELECT id, username, password FROM users
   WHERE username = '".$_POST['username'].'"')or die(mysql_error( ));
   // Set the user account number
   $row = mysql_fetch_object($check);
   $acn = $row->id;
   // Set a variable to the user name
   $uname = $_POST['username'];
   // Set a variable to the user password
   $upword = $_POST['pass'];
   break;
  } // End ifelse
 } // End while
```

```
?>
```

6. Write the user account number to a file called p.tmp on the client computer. Post menu options for the PDCRS to the user.

```php
<?php
// Write the user account to a temporary file
$ffile = 'p.tmp';
$fp = fopen ($ffile, 'w');
fputs ($fp, $acn);
fclose ($fp);
// Display user options in the PDCRS
echo '<center><h1>Update User Profile</h1></center><br>';
echo '<h3>User Profile</h3>';
echo "<a href= 'pfile.php'>Click Here to Update User Profile</a>";
echo '<h3>User Profile Reports</h3>';
echo "<a href='iprorpt.php'>Click Here for Individual User Profile Report</a><br>";
echo "<a href='aprorpt.php'>Click Here for All Users Profile Report</a><br>";
echo '<center><h1>Update Performance Data</h1></center><br>';
echo '<h3>Performance Data</h3>';
echo "<a href= 'dfile.php'>Click Here to Update Performance Data</a>";
echo '<h3>Performance Data Reports</h3>';
echo "<a href='iprpt.php'>Click Here for Individual Organization Performance Report</a><br>";
echo "<a href='aprpt.php'>Click Here for All Organizations Performance Report</a><br>";
?>
</body>
</html>
```

5.4. User Profile in the PDCRS

Registered users may store profile data. These data are used to define ownership for the user's data. Data stored in the PDCRS are stored and changed by the owners of the data. An owner of data in the PDCRS is a user that stored the data in the user assigned account associated with that user's identification and password.

Registered PDCRS user profile data are stored in a database table called profile. An SQL command that created the profile table is detailed in Figure 42.

CREATE TABLE profile (ID MEDIUMINT NOT NULL AUTO_INCREMENT PRIMARY KEY,
    fname   VARCHAR(30),lname   VARCHAR(30),   address   VARCHAR(35),
city VARCHAR(35), state VARCHAR(2), zipcode VARCHAR(10), phone
VARCHAR(10), email VARCHAR(60))
Figure 42. Create a PDCRS User Profile Table

5.4.1. User Profile Form Fields

User profile data are first name, last name, email address or user identification code,
password, address, city, State, zip code, and telephone number. A form in Figure 43
details the fields in the user profile form.

```
echo '<form action="upfile.php" method="post">';
echo "<table border='0'>";
echo '<tr><td colspan=2><h1>User Profile</h1></td></tr>';
echo '<tr><td>First Name:</td><td>';
echo "<input type='text' name='fname' value='$fname' maxlength='30'>";
echo '</td></tr>';
echo '<tr><td>Last Name:</td><td>';
echo "<input type='text' name='lname' value='$lname' maxlength='30'>";
echo '</td></tr>';
echo '<tr><td>Address:</td><td>';
echo "<input type='text' name='address' value='$address' maxlength='35'>";
echo '</td></tr>';
echo '<tr><td>City:</td><td>';
echo "<input type='text' name='city' value='$city' maxlength='35'>";
echo '</td></tr>';
echo '<tr><td>State:</td><td>';
echo "<input type='text' name='state' value='$state' maxlength='2'>";
echo '</td></tr>';
echo '<tr><td>Zipcode:</td><td>';
echo "<input type='text' name='zipcode' value='$zipcode' maxlength='10'>";
echo '</td></tr>';
echo '<tr><td>Phone:</td><td>';
echo "<input type='text' name='phone' value='$phone' maxlength='10'>";
echo '</td></tr>';
echo '<tr><td>Email:</td><td>';
```

```
echo "<input type='text' name='email' value='$email' maxlength='60'>";
echo '</td></tr>';
echo '<tr><td>  </td><td>';
echo "<input type='hidden' name='passme' value='$acn' maxlength='10'>";
echo '</td></tr>';
echo "<tr><td colspan='2' align='right'>";
echo "<input type='submit' value='Profile'>";
echo '</td></tr>';
echo '</table>';
echo ' </form>';
```
Figure 43. User Profile Form

5.4.2. Store, Retrieve, and Update User Profile Data

User profile data forms are implemented to store, retrieve, and update data. The data in the PDCRS profile data are stored and updated by the owners of the data. User profile data store form is implemented with a script detailed in Figure 45. A retrieve and update form script is implemented with Figure 44. A PDCRS profile data script to retrieve and update the profile table is detailed with a range of steps:

1. Start a profile web page and set the page color. Set PHP to be executed on the server.
```
<!-- ----------------------- -->
<!-- Update User Profile -->
<!-- ----------------------- -->
<html>
<!-- Set the HTML page color -->
<body  BGCOLOR=#D66321>
<?php
```
2. Read the user account number from the temporary file. Connect the user to the MySQL database server and set the database to the PDCRS database pdcrs.
```
// Read  the user account number
$ffile = 'p.tmp';
$fp = fopen ($ffile, 'r');
$acn = fgets($fp);
fclose ($fp);
echo '<center><h1>Update User Profile</h1></center><br>';
// Connect to the PDCRS database
mysql_connect('localhost', 'pdcrs', '  ') or die(mysql_error( ));
```

mysql_select_db('pdcrs') or die(mysql_error( ));

3. Query the profile table for the user profile data based on the user account. Initialize and post the profile form to the user in the client browser. The current user profile data are posted in the user browser. Any form data field may be changed. The user saves the profile field changes by clicking the submit button defined as Profile. Control transfers to Figure 44 to process the profile form action script.

```
// Read the User Profile Record
$allp = "select id, fname, lname, address, city, state, zipcode, phone, email from profile where id = '$acn'";
$check = mysql_query("$allp") or die("Invalid Select Profile query: ".mysql_error( ));
$row = mysql_fetch_object($check);
$fname = $row->fname; $lname = $row->lname; $address = $row->address; $city = $row->city;
$state = $row->state; $zipcode = $row->zipcode; $phone = $row->phone; $email = $row->email;
// User profile form
echo '<form action="upfile.php" method="post">';
echo "<table border='0'>";
echo '<tr><td colspan=2><h1>User Profile</h1></td></tr>';
echo '<tr><td>First Name:</td><td>';
echo "<input type='text' name='fname' value='$fname' maxlength='30'>";
echo '</td></tr>';
echo '<tr><td>Last Name:</td><td>';
echo "<input type='text' name='lname' value='$lname' maxlength='30'>";
echo '</td></tr>';
echo '<tr><td>Address:</td><td>';
echo "<input type='text' name='address' value='$address' maxlength='35'>";
echo '</td></tr>';
echo '<tr><td>City:</td><td>';
echo "<input type='text' name='city' value='$city' maxlength='35'>";
echo '</td></tr>';
echo '<tr><td>State:</td><td>';
echo "<input type='text' name='state' value='$state' maxlength='2'>";
echo '</td></tr>';
echo '<tr><td>Zipcode:</td><td>';
echo "<input type='text' name='zipcode' value='$zipcode' maxlength='10'>";
```

```
echo '</td></tr>';
echo '<tr><td>Phone:</td><td>';
echo "<input type='text' name='phone' value='$phone' maxlength='10'>";
echo '</td></tr>';
echo '<tr><td>Email:</td><td>';
echo "<input type='text' name='email' value='$email' maxlength='60'>";
echo '</td></tr>';
echo '<tr><td> </td><td>';
echo "<input type='hidden' name='passme' value='$acn' maxlength='10'>";
echo '</td></tr>';
echo "<tr><td colspan='2' align='right'>";
echo "<input type='submit' value='Profile'>";
echo '</td></tr>';
echo '</table>';
echo ' </form>';
?>
</body>
</html>
```
Figure 44. User Profile Retrieve and Update Script

5.4.3. User Profile Form Action Script

This profile form action script is executed after a user press the Profile button in Figure 43. Profile form data are stored in the profile table with a range of steps:

1. Start a web page and set the page color.

```
<html>
<body BGCOLOR=#D66321>
<center><h1>User Profile Updated</h></center><br><br>
```
2. Set PHP to execute the script on the server. Connect the PDCRS to the MySQL server and set the PDCRS database to pdcrs.
```
<?php
// Connect to the PDCRS database
mysql_connect('localhost', 'pdcrs', '  ') or die(mysql_error( ));
mysql_select_db('pdcrs') or die(mysql_error( ));
```
3. Retrieve the profile form data and update or store the data in the profile table. Post a menu option to return to the PDCRS home page.
```
$fn = $_POST['fname'];  $ln = $_POST['lname'];  $ad = $_POST['address'];
$ct = $_POST['city'];  $st = $_POST['state'];  $zi = $_POST['zipcode'];
```

```
$ph = $_POST['phone'];  $em = $_POST['email']; $dd = $_POST['passme'];
$udate = "Update profile set fname = '$fn',lname = '$ln', address = '$ad',city = '$ct',
state = '$st', zipcode = '$zi', phone = '$ph', email = '$em' where ID = '$dd' ";
mysql_query("$udate") or die("Invalid Insertion Profile query: ".mysql_error( ));
echo '<h3>Return to Home Page</h3>';
echo '<a href= "index.html">Click Here for Home Page</a>';
?>
</body>
</html>
```
Figure 45. User Profile Store Script

5.5. Performance Data

Registered PDCRS user performance data are stored in a database table called pdata. An SQL command that created the pdata table is detailed in Figure 46.

```
CREATE TABLE pdata (ID MEDIUMINT NOT NULL AUTO_INCREMENT
PRIMARY KEY,
 orgname VARCHAR(35), bestpra VARCHAR(254), numprod DECIMAL(6),
prodsale DECIMAL(10,2), numemp DECIMAL(6), modayr DATE)
```
Figure 46. Create a Performance Data Table

5.5.1. Performance Data Form Fields

Performance data fields are organization name, best practices number of products, product sale revenues, number of employees, month, day, and year. The form fields implement technologies that minimize keyboard input. Drop down list, radio buttons, check boxes, and other form point and click techniques are used for data input. Figure 47 details a performance data form.

```
echo '<form action="upfile.php" method="post">';
echo "<table border='0'>";
echo '<tr><td colspan=2><h1>User Profile</h1></td></tr>';
echo '<tr><td>First Name:</td><td>';
echo "<input type='text' name='fname' value='$fname' maxlength='30'>";
echo '</td></tr>';
echo '<tr><td>Last Name:</td><td>';
echo "<input type='text' name='lname' value='$lname' maxlength='30'>";
echo '</td></tr>';
echo '<tr><td>Address:</td><td>';
```

```
echo "<input type='text' name='address' value='$address' maxlength='35'>";
echo '</td></tr>';
echo '<tr><td>City:</td><td>';
echo "<input type='text' name='city' value='$city' maxlength='35'>";
echo '</td></tr>';
echo '<tr><td>State:</td><td>';
echo "<input type='text' name='state' value='$state' maxlength='2'>";
echo '</td></tr>';
echo '<tr><td>Zipcode:</td><td>';
echo "<input type='text' name='zipcode' value='$zipcode' maxlength='10'>";
echo '</td></tr>';
echo '<tr><td>Phone:</td><td>';
echo "<input type='text' name='phone' value='$phone' maxlength='10'>";
echo '</td></tr>';
echo '<tr><td>Email:</td><td>';
echo "<input type='text' name='email' value='$email' maxlength='60'>";
echo '</td></tr>';
echo '<tr><td> </td><td>';
echo "<input type='hidden' name='passme' value='$acn' maxlength='10'>",
echo '</td></tr>';
echo "<tr><td colspan='2' align='right'>";
echo "<input type='submit' value='Profile'>";
echo '</td></tr>';
echo '</table>';
echo ' </form>';
```
Figure 47. Performance Data Form

5.5.2. Store, Retrieve, and Update Performance Data

Performance data forms are implemented to store, retrieve, and update data. The data in the PDCRS performance data are stored and updated by the owners of the data. The performance data store form is implemented with a script detailed in Figure 49. Retrieve and update form script is implemented with Figure 48. A PDCRS performance data script to retrieve and update the pdata table is detailed with a range of steps in Section 5.5.2.1.

5.5.2.1. Performance Data Retrieve Script

1. Start a performance data web page and set the page color. Set PHP to be executed on the server.

```
<!-- ------------------------------- -->
<!-- Update Performance Data -->
<!-- ------------------------------- -->
<html>
<!-- Set the HTML page color -->
<body  BGCOLOR=#D66321>
<?php
```

2. Read the user account number from the temporary file. Connect the user to the MySQL database server and set the database to the PDCRS database pdcrs.

```
// Read  the user account number
$ffile = 'p.tmp';
$fp = fopen ($ffile, 'r');
$acn = fgets($fp);
fclose ($fp);
echo '<center><h1>Update Performance Data</h1></center><br>';
// Connect to the PDCRS database
mysql_connect ('localhost', 'pdcrs', '  ') or die(mysql_error( ));
mysql_select_db('pdcrs') or die(mysql_error( ));
```

3. Query the pdata table for the user performance data based on the user account. Initialize and post the performance data form to the user in the client browser. The current user performance data are posted in the user browser. Any form data field may be changed. The user saves the performance data field changes by clicking the submit button defined as Performance. Control transfers to Figure 48 to process the performance data form action script.

```
// Read the User Profile Record
$allp = "select id, orgname, bestpra, numprod, prodsale, numemp, modayr from pdata where id = '$acn'";
$check = mysql_query("$allp") or die("Invalid Select Profile query: ".mysql_error( ));
$row = mysql_fetch_object($check);
$orgname = $row->orgname; $bestpra = $row->bestpra; $numprod = $row->numprod; $prodsale = $row->prodsale;
$numemp = $row->numemp; $modayr = $row->modayr;
```

```
// Performance data form
echo '<form action="updfile.php" method="post">';
echo "<table border='0'>";
echo '<tr><td colspan=2><h1>Performance Data</h1></td></tr>';
echo '<tr><td>Organization Name:</td><td>';
echo "<input type='text' name='orgname' value='$orgname' maxlength='35'>";
echo '</td></tr>';
echo '<tr><td>Best Pratices:</td><td>';
echo "<TEXTAREA name='bestpra' COLS='25' ROWS='10'
WRAP='VIRTUAL'>$bestpra</TEXTAREA>";
echo '</td></tr>';
echo '<tr><td>Number of Products:</td><td>';
echo "<input type='text' name='numprod' value='$numprod' maxlength='6'>";
echo '</td></tr>';
echo '<tr><td>Product Sales Revenues:</td><td>';
echo "<input type='text' name='prodsale' value='$prodsale' maxlength='10'>";
echo '</td></tr>';
echo '<tr><td>Number of Employees:</td><td>';
echo "<input type='text' name='numemp' value='$numemp' maxlength='6'>";
echo '</td></tr>';
echo '<tr><td>Year-Month-Day (2006-11-25):</td><td>';
echo "<input type='text' name='modayr' value='$modayr' maxlength='10'>";
echo '</td></tr>';
echo '<tr><td> </td><td>';
echo "<input type='hidden' name='passme' value='$acn' maxlength='10'>";
echo '</td></tr>';
echo "<tr><td colspan='2' align='right'>";
echo "<input type='submit' value='Performance'>";
echo '</td></tr>';
echo '</table>';
echo ' </form>';
?>
</body>
</html>
```

Figure 48. Performance Data Retrieve and Update Script

5.5.2.2. Performance Data Form Action Script

This performance data form action script is executed after a user press the Performance button in Figure 48. Performance form data are stored in the pdata table with a range of steps:

1. Start a web page and set the page color.
```
<html>
<body BGCOLOR=#D66321>
<center><h1>Performance Data Updated</h></center><br><br>
```

2. Set PHP to execute the script on the server. Connect the PDCRS to the MySQL server and set the PDCRS database to pdcrs.
```
<?php
// Connect to the PDCRS database
mysql_connect('localhost', 'pdcrs', ' ') or die(mysql_error( ));
mysql_select_db('pdcrs') or die(mysql_error( ));
```

3. Retrieve the performance form data and update or store the data in the pdata table. Post a menu option to return to the PDCRS home page.
```
$or = $_POST['orgname']; $be = $_POST['bestpra']; $np = $_
POST['numprod'];
$pr = $_POST['prodsale']; $ne = $_POST['numemp'];  $mo = $_
POST['modayr'];
$dd = $_POST['passme'];
$udate = "Update pdata set orgname = '$or',bestpra = '$be', numprod =
'$np',prodsale = '$pr',
numemp = '$ne', modayr = '$mo' where ID = '$dd' ";
mysql_query("$udate") or die("Invalid Insertion Profile query: ".mysql_error( ));
echo '<h3>Return to Home Page</h3>';
echo '<a href= "index.html">Click Here for Home Page</a>';
?>
</body>
</html>
```
Figure 49. Performance Data Store Script

5.6. Performance Reports

A list of performance reports is posted for the users of the PDCRS. Each report is discussed with a script file. Reports are posted in the user client machine browser with an option to return to the PDCRS home page. PDCRS report scripts are detailed with a range of steps.

5.6.1. Individual User Profile Report

1. Start a web page and set the page color.

```
<!-- ----------------------- -->
<!-- User Profile Report -->
<!-- ----------------------- -->
<html>
<!-- Set the HTML page color -->
<body  BGCOLOR=#D66321>
```

2. Set PHP to execute script code on the server. Read the user account number from the user computer. Connect the user to the MySQL database server and set the PDCRS database to pdcrs.

```
<?php
// Read  the user account number
$ffile = 'p.tmp';
$fp = fopen ($ffile, 'r');
$acn = fgets ($fp);
fclose ($fp);
echo '<center><h1>Individual User Profile Report</h1></center><br>';
// Connect to the PDCRS database
mysql_connect('localhost', 'pdcrs', '  ') or die(mysql_error( ));
mysql_select_db('pdcrs') or die(mysql_error( ));
```

3. Retrieve the user profile record in a record set.

```
// Read the User Profile Record
$allp = "select id, fname, lname, address, city, state, zipcode, phone, email from profile where id = '$acn'";
$result = mysql_query("$allp") or die("Invalid Select Profile query: ".mysql_error( ));
$row = mysql_fetch_object($result);
```

4. Extract user profile data from the record set.

```
$fname = $row->fname; $lname = $row->lname; $address = $row->address; $city = $row->city;
```

$state = $row->state; $zipcode = $row->zipcode; $phone = $row->phone; $email = $row->email;

5. Post the user profile data in a table.

```
echo '<table border>';
// Table column headers
echo '<tr>';
echo '<th>First</th>';
echo '<th>Last</th>';
echo '<th>Address</th>';
echo '<th>City</th>';
echo '<th>State</th>';
echo '<th>Zipcode</th>';
echo '<th>Phone</th>';
echo '<th>Email</th>';
echo '</tr>';
// Table column data content
echo '<tr>';
echo "<td>$fname</td>";
echo "<td>$lname</td>";
echo "<td>$address</td>";
echo "<td>$city</td>";
echo "<td>$state</td>";
echo "<td>$zipcode</td>";
echo "<td>$phone</td>";
echo "<td>$email</td>";
echo '</tr>';
echo '</table>';
?>
<h3>Return to Home Page</h3>
<a href="index.html">Click Here for Home Page</a>
</body>
</html>
```

5.6.2. All User Profile Report

1. Start a web page and set the page color.

```
<!-- ----------------------- -->
```

```
<!-- User Profile Report -->
<!-- ---------------------- -->
<html>
<!-- Set the HTML page color -->
<body  BGCOLOR=#D66321>
```

2. Set PHP to execute script code on the server. Read the user account number from the user computer. Connect the user to the MySQL database server and set the PDCRS database to pdcrs.

```php
<?php
// Read  the user account number
$ffile = 'p.tmp';
$fp = fopen ($ffile, 'r');
$acn = fgets ($fp);
fclose ($fp);
echo '<center><h1>All User Profile Report</h1></center><br>';
// Connect to the PDCRS database
mysql_connect ('localhost', 'pdcrs', '  ') or die(mysql_error( ));
mysql_select_db ('pdcrs') or die(mysql_error( ));
```

3. Retrieve the all profile records in a record set.

```php
// Read the User Profile Record
$allp = "select id, fname, lname, address, city, state, zipcode, phone, email from profile";
$result = mysql_query("$allp") or die("Invalid Select Profile query: ".mysql_error( ));
$row = mysql_fetch_object($result);
```

4. Post the user profile data in a table.

```php
echo '<table border>';
// Table column header
echo '<tr>';
echo '<th>First</th>';
echo '<th>Last</th>';
echo '<th>Address</th>';
echo '<th>City</th>';
echo '<th>State</th>';
echo '<th>Zipcode</th>';
echo '<th>Phone</th>';
```

```
echo '<th>Email</th>';
echo '</tr>';
```

5. Extract user profile data fields by rows from the record set.
```
// Fetch rows in reverse order
for ($i = mysql_num_rows($result) - 1; $i >= 0; $i--)
 { if (!mysql_data_seek($result, $i))
    { echo "Cannot seek to row $i:" . mysql_error( ) . "\n";
      continue;
    } // End Row If
  if (!($row = mysql_fetch_object($result)))
    continue;
  echo '<tr>';
  echo "<td>$row->fname</td>";
  echo "<td>$row->lname</td>";
  echo "<td>$row->address</td>";
  echo "<td>$row->city</td>";
  echo "<td>$row->state</td>";
  echo "<td>$row->zipcode</td>";
  echo "<td>$row->phone</td>";
  echo "<td>$row->email</td>";
  echo '</tr>';
} // End for
echo '</table>';
?>
<h3>Return to Home Page</h3>
<a href="index.html">Click Here for Home Page</a>
</body>
</html>
```

5.6.3. Individual User Performance Data Report

1. Start a web page and set the page color.
```
<!-- ---------------------------------------------------- -->
<!-- Individual User Performance Data Report -->
<!-- ---------------------------------------------------- -->
<html>
<!-- Set the HTML page color -->
```

```
<body BGCOLOR=#D66321>
```

2. Set PHP to execute script code on the server. Read the user account number from the user computer. Connect the user to the MySQL database server and set the PDCRS database to pdcrs.

```php
<?php
// Read  the user account number
$ffile = 'p.tmp';
$fp = fopen ($ffile, 'r');
$acn = fgets ($fp);
fclose ($fp);
echo '<center><h1>Individual Performance Data Report</h1></center><br>';
// Connect to the PDCRS database
mysql_connect('localhost', 'pdcrs', '  ') or die(mysql_error( ));
mysql_select_db('pdcrs') or die(mysql_error( ));
```

3. Retrieve the user performance data record in a record set.

```php
// Read the User Performance Data Record
$allp = "select id, orgname, bestpra, numprod, prodsale, numemp, modayr from
pdata where id = '$acn'";
$result = mysql_query("$allp") or die("Invalid Select Profile query: ".mysql_error( ));
$row = mysql_fetch_object($result);
```

4. Extract user performance data from the record set.

```php
$orgname = $row->orgname; $bestpra = $row->bestpra; $numprod = $row-
>numprod; $prodsale = $row->prodsale;
$numemp = $row->numemp; $modayr = $row->modayr;
```

5. Post the performance data in a table.

```php
echo '<table border>';
echo '<tr>';
echo '<th>Organization</th>';
echo '<th>Best Pratice</th>';
echo '<th>No. of Products</th>';
echo '<th>Product Sales</th>';
echo '<th>No. of Employees</th>';
echo '<th>Date</th>';
echo '</tr>';
echo '<tr>';
```

```
echo "<td>$orgname</td>";
echo "<td>$bestpra</td>";
echo "<td>$numprod</td>";
echo "<td>$prodsale</td>";
echo "<td>$numemp</td>";
echo "<td>$modayr</td>";
echo '</tr>';
echo '</table>';
?>
<h3>Return to Home Page</h3>
<a href="index.html">Click Here for Home Page</a>
</body>
</html>
```

5.6.4. All User Performance Data Report

1. Start a web page and set the page color.
```
<!-- ----------------------------------------- -->
<!-- All User Performance Data Report -->
<!-- ----------------------------------------- -->
<html>
<!-- Set the HTML page color -->
<body  BGCOLOR=#D66321>
```

2. Set PHP to execute script code on the server. Read the user account number from the user computer. Connect the user to the MySQL database server and set the PDCRS database to pdcrs.
```
<?php
// Read  the user account number
$ffile = 'p.tmp';
$fp = fopen ($ffile, 'r');
$acn = fgets($fp);
fclose ($fp);
echo '<center><h1>All User Performance Data Report</h1></center><br>';
// Connect to the PDCRS database
mysql_connect('localhost', 'pdcrs', ' ') or die(mysql_error( ));
mysql_select_db('pdcrs') or die(mysql_error( ));
```

3. Retrieve all user performance data records in a record set.
// Read the User Performance data Record
$allp = "select id, orgname, bestpra, numprod, prodsale, numemp, modayr from pdata";
$result = mysql_query("$allp") or die("Invalid Select Profile query: ".mysql_error( ));
$row = mysql_fetch_object($result);

4. Post the performance data in table.
echo '<table border>';
// Table column header
echo '<tr>';
echo '<th>Organization</th>';
echo '<th>Best Pratice</th>';
echo '<th>No. of Products</th>';
echo '<th>Product Sales</th>';
echo '<th>No. of Employees</th>';
echo '<th>Date</th>';
echo '</tr>';

5. Extract user performance data by fields in rows from the record set.
// Fetch rows in reverse order
for ($i = mysql_num_rows($result) - 1; $i >= 0; $i--)
 { if (!mysql_data_seek($result, $i))
    { echo "Cannot seek to row $i:" . mysql_error( ) . "\n";
      continue;
    } // End Row If
  if (!($row = mysql_fetch_object($result)))
    continue;
  echo '<tr>';
  echo "<td>$row->orgname</td>";
  echo "<td>$row->bestpra</td>";
  echo "<td>$row->numprod</td>";
  echo "<td>$row->prodsale</td>";
  echo "<td>$row->numemp</td>";
  echo "<td>$row->modayr</td>";
  echo '</tr>';
} // End for
echo '</table>';
?>
<h3>Return to Home Page</h3>

```
<a href="index.html">Click Here for Home Page</a>
</body>
</html>
```

5.7. Application Root

The application root for the PDCRS is an HTML file called index.html stored on the server. The user accesses this file from the client machine through the browser to run the PDCRS application on the server. When the application starts two links are visible. The Register User link manages the user identification and password in the PDCRS users table. Each registered user is assigned an account number by the PDCRS. Login User link manages the user access to PDCRS recourses. A root HTML document called index.html is detailed in Figure 50.

```
<html>
<body BGCOLOR=#D66321>
<center><h1>Performance Data Collection and Reports</h1></center>
<a href="reguser.php">Register User</a><br>
<a href="loguser.php">Login</a><br>
</body>
</html>
```
Figure 50. Index.html Root for PDCRS

5.8. Application MySQL Database Dump

An implemented client/server application was detailed in Chapter 5. The MySQL database may be loaded from a database dump. At the administration level on a computer running the MySQL Server a database is dumped with a database dump command.

```
mysqldump –u  -p --databases name > name.sql,
```
where name is the database to be dumped.

The pdcrs MySQL database dump for the PDCRS is detailed in Appendix H.

A MySQL database is loaded with a MySQL database load command.

```
loadbatch < name.sql
```

The database dump file is name.sql.

5.9. Exercises

1. Use the SQL dump in Appendix H to setup the users, profile, and pdata tables on a MySQL database server running the PHP script language.

2. Create the users, profile, and pdata tables with SQL statements from Sections 5.3, 5.4, and 5.5.

3. Install the PDCRS script files on a MySQL server running with PHP after exercise 1 and 2 are completed. Edit the PHP script files and change the pdcrs PDCRS database name to your database name. The database name pdcrs occurs one time in each script that connects the user to the MySQL database server. Test the installed PDCRS by running a browser on a client machine connected to your MySQL database server.

4. Make changes to the PDCRS implemented on the MySQL server. Insert a picture on the home page. Change the web pages to different colors.

5. Generate new reports from the table columns in the performance data table called pdata. Generate numerical aggregates from the numeric fields in the pdata table.

6. Generate new reports from columns in the users and profile table for individual and all users in the PDCRS. Generate new reports from columns in the profile and pdata tables for individual and all users in the PDCRS.

7. Create at least three tables with character or string and numeric data to define additional performance data.

8. Implement forms that include radio buttons, check boxes, menus, and active images for each table created in exercise 7.

9. Implement PHP scripts to interface with the PDCRS user's client machines to input, update, and store data in each table created in exercise 7.

10. Implement PHP scripts to interface with the PDCRS user's client machines to generate single table and multiple table reports to aggregate the performance statistics.

11. Dump your MySQL database after exercises 1 through 10 are implemented.

References

1. Lyman Ott, An Introduction to Statistical Methods and Data Analysis, Duxbury Press, 1977.

2. Edward Hill, Jr., A Comparative Study of Very Large Databases, Lecture Notes in Computer Science, Volume No. 59, Springer-Verlag, 1978.

3. D. E. Knuth, The Art of Computer Programming, Volume 3, Searching and Sorting, Addison-Wesley Publishing Company, Reading, Mass., 1973.

4. T. C. Lowe, The Influence of Data Base Characteristics and Usage on Direct Access File Organization, J. ACM, 15, 4 (Oct. 1968) pp. 535-548.

5. G. K. Zipf, Human Behavior and The Principle of Least Effort, Hafner Publishing Company, (1965).

6. Charles A. Olson, Random Access File Organization for Indirectly Addressed Records, Advanced Applications, Inc., San Francisco, California.

7. Elizabeth Castro, Perl and CGI for the World Wide Web: Visual QuickStart Guide , Second Edition, http://www.peachpit.com, 2001.

8. D. E. Knuth, J. H. Morris, Jr., and V. R. Pratt, Fast Pattern Matching in Strings, SIAM JKournal opn Computing, Volume 6, No. 1, pp. 323-350, 1977.

9. Edward Hill, Jr., First Course: Data Structures and Algorithms Using Java, iUniverse, Inc., 2004.

10. Edward Hill, Jr., Learning to Program Java, iUniverse, Inc., 2005.

11. Andi Gutmans, Stig Saether Bakken, and Derick Rethans, PHP 5 Power Programming, Prentice Hall, 2005.

12. Paul Dubois, Stefan Hinz, Carsten Pedersen, MySQL Certification Study Guide, MySQL Press, 2004.

13. Elizabeth Castro, HTML For The World Wide Web, Peachpit Press, 1997.

14. class   Vector,   http://java.sun.com/j2se/1.4.2/docs/api/java/util/Vector.html, 2007.

15. HTML Tutorial, http://www.w3schools.com/html/default.asp, 2007.

16. PHP Tutorial, http://www.w3schools.com/html/default.asp, 2007.

17. MySQL   Tutorial,   http://www.devshed.com/c/a/MySQL/Beginning-MySQL-Tutorial/, 2007.

Appendix A
List Abstract Data Type

```
// ------------------------------------------------------------------
// Version 1.26: Class ListNode and class List definitions
// ------------------------------------------------------------------
import javax.swing.*;
import java.io.*;
class ListNode {
// package access data so class List can access it directly
Object data; Object data1, data2, data3, data4;
ListNode next;
ListNode prev;
ListNode ptr;
// ------------------------------------------------------------
// Constructor: Create a ListNode that refers to Object o.
// Make the next or link address null
// ------------------------------------------------------------
ListNode (Object o) { this (o, null); }

// -------------------------------------------------------------------
// Constructor: Create a ListNode that refers to Object o and
// to the next ListNode in the List.
// nextNode is a pointer to the next node
// -------------------------------------------------------------------
ListNode (Object o, ListNode nextNode)
{
   data = o;        // this node refers to Object o
   next = nextNode; // set next to refer to next
   prev = null;
   ptr = null;
}
```

```
// -----------------------------------------------------
// Return a reference to the Object in this node
// -----------------------------------------------------
Object getObject (int i)
{Object tmp = data;
 switch (i)
  {case 0: tmp = data; break;
   case 1: tmp = data1; break;
   case 2: tmp = data2; break;
   case 3: tmp = data3; break;
   case 4: tmp = data4; break;
   }
 return tmp;
 }


// --------------------------------------------------
// Return the next node pointer or address
// --------------------------------------------------
ListNode getNext ( ) { return next; }
}

// ------------------------
// Class List definition
// ------------------------
public class List
{
private String name;  // String like "list" used in printing

// Constructor: Construct an empty List with s as the name
public List (String s)
{
 name = s;
}
// -----------------------------------------------------
// Constructor: Construct an empty List with
// "list" as the name
// -----------------------------------------------------
public List ( )
{ this ("list");
```

```
}

public synchronized Object info(ListNode ptr, int i)
{// Return the info from a node pointed to by ptr
Object tmp = ptr.data;
  switch (i)
  { case 0: tmp = ptr.data; break;
    case 1: tmp = ptr.data1; break;
    case 2: tmp = ptr.data2; break;
    case 3: tmp = ptr.data3; break;
    case 4: tmp = ptr.data4; break;
  }
  return tmp;
}
public synchronized void infoi (ListNode ptr, Object K, int i)
{ // Insert the info K into a node pointed to by ptr

  switch (i)
  { case 0: ptr.data = K;
    case 1: ptr.data1 = K; break;
    case 2: ptr.data2 = K; break;
    case 3: ptr.data3 = K; break;
    case 4: ptr.data4 = K; break;
  }
}
public synchronized ListNode CDR (ListNode ptt)
{
  return ptt.next;
}
public synchronized ListNode LCDR (ListNode ptt)
{
  return ptt.prev;
}
public synchronized void CONS (ListNode ptt, ListNode pti)
{// Connect the new node pointed to by pti to the right link of
 // a node pointed to by ptt
  ptt.next = pti;
}
public synchronized void LCONS (ListNode ptt, ListNode pti)
```

```
{// Connect the new node pointed to by pti to the left link of
 // a node pointed to by ptt
   ptt.prev = pti;
}
public synchronized void ptosi (ListNode sn, ListNode ptrr)
{ // Insert the pointer info in the node
   sn.ptr = ptrr;
}
public synchronized ListNode ptoso (ListNode sn)
{ // Return the pointer info from the node
   return sn.ptr;
}


// ------------------------------------------------------------
// Place all your methods for the implementation of the
// algorithms in this section of the code
// Note:  The code above must not be altered.
// ------------------------------------------------------------
//
// ****** Do not make any code changes above this line ***
// ************************************************
// Insert User Java methods and Java public static void main
// ************************************************
} // End List Class ADT
```

Appendix B
An Input/Output Example

```java
import javax.swing.*;
import java.io.*;
class iobuf
{
//--------------------------------
// Setup File Reference Handle
//--------------------------------
private BufferedReader Ibuf (String filename)
throws java.io.IOException
{
  // Setup the basic input stream
  FileReader fr = new FileReader (filename);
  // Buffer the input stream
  BufferedReader br = new BufferedReader (fr);
  return br;
} // End Ibuf


//----------------------
// Input a Data Item
//----------------------
public static String Inf (BufferedReader br)
throws java.io.IOException
{ String inval;

  if ((inval = br.readLine ( )) != null)
    {
      return inval;
    } else return null;

} // End Inf
```

```java
public static void main (String args [ ])
 throws java.io.IOException
 { // Delcare Variables
   String foo = "AA";
   int Total=0;
   // Define a Reference Variable to the Container
   iobuf  DL = new iobuf ( );
   BufferedReader tk;
   // Set the Path and Input File Name
   String FName = "C:\\spring2004\\csc426\\INFO.DAT";

   // Setup file reference handle
   tk = DL.Ibuf (FName);

   // Read an Input Data Items One-at-a-Time
   while (foo != null)
   { // Input Data and Return String Data Value
     foo = DL.Inf (tk);

     // Add to Total
     if (foo != null) Total = Total + Integer.parseInt (foo);

     // Post GUI With Data
     JOptionPane.showMessageDialog (null,"Value = "+foo);
   } // End while

   // Post Total Value
   JOptionPane.showMessageDialog (null,"Total of all Information = "+Total);

   // Close the Input File
   tk.close ( );

   // Terminate Program
   System.exit (0);

 } // End Method main
} // iobuf
```

Appendix C
Class Vector Information

Table 1. class Vector Field Summary

Field Type and Name	Description
protected int capacityIncrement	The amount by which the capacity of the vector is automatically incremented when its size becomes greater than its capacity.
protected int elementCount	The number of valid components in this Vector object.
protected Object [ ] elementData	The array buffer into which the components of the vector are stored.

Table 2. class Vector Constructor Summary

Constructor Name	Description
Vector ( )	Constructs an empty vector so that its internal data Array has size 10 and its standard capacity increment is zero.
Vector (Collection c)	Constructs a vector containing the elements of the specified collection, in the order they are returned by the collection's iterator. Parameters: c—the collection whose elements are to be placed into this vector. Throws: **NullPointerException**—if the specified collection is null.
Vector	Constructs an empty vector with the specified

| (int initialCapacity) | initial capacity and with its capacity increment equal to zero.
Parameters:
initialCapacity—the initial capacity of the vector.
Throws:
IllegalArgumentException—if the specified initial capacity is negative. |
| Vector (int initialCapacity,
int capacityIncrement) | Constructs an empty vector with the specified initial capacity and capacity increment.
Parameters: |

Table 2. class Vector Constructor Summary-Cont

Constructor Name	Description
	initialCapacity—the initial capacity of the vector. capacityIncrement—the amount by which the capacity is increased when the vector overflows. Throws: **IllegalArgumentException** - if the specified initial capacity is negative.

Table 3. class Vector Method Summary

Type	Method Name	Description
void	add (int index, Object element)	Inserts the specified element at the specified position in this Vector. Shifts the element currently at that position (if any) and anysubsequent elements to the right (adds one to t heir indices). Specified by: **add** in interface **List** Overrides: **add** in class **AbstractList** Parameters:

		index—index at which the specified element is to be inserted.
		element—ielement to be inserted.
		Throws:
		ArrayIndexOutOfBounds Exception —index is out of range (index < 0 || index > size( )).
boolean add	Object o)	Appends the specified element to the end of this Vector.
		Specified by:
		add in interface **List**
		Overrides:
		add in class **AbstractList**
		Parameters:
		o—element to be appended to this Vector.
		Returns:
		true (as per the general contract of Collection.add).
boolean	addAll (Collection c)	Appends all of the elements in the specified Collection to the end of this Vector, in the order that they are returned by the specified

Table 3. class Vector Method Summary-Cont

Type	Method Name	Description
		Collection's Iterator. The behavior of this operation is undefined if the specified Collection is modified while the operation is in progress. (This implies that the behavior of this call is undefined if the specified Collection is this Vector, and this Vector is nonempty.)
		Specified by:

addAll in interface **List**
Overrides:
addAll in class **Abstract Collection**
Parameters:
c—elements to be inserted into this Vector.
Returns:
true if this Vector changed as a result of the call.
Throws:
NullPointerException—if the specified
collection is null.

boolean	addAll (int index, Collection c)

Inserts all of the elements in in the specified Collection into this Vector at the specified position. Shifts the element currently at that position (if any) and any subsequent elements to the right (increases their indices). The new elements will appear in the Vector in the order that they are returned by the specified Collection's iterator.
Specified by:
addAll in interface **List**
Overrides:
addAll in class **AbstractList**
Parameters:
index—index at which to insert first element
from the specified collection.
c—elements to be inserted into this Vector.
Returns:
true if this Vector changed as a result of the call.

| | | Throws:
ArrayIndexOutOfBounds
Exception—index
out of range (index < 0 \|\| index >
size( )).
NullPointerException—if the
specified |

Table 3. class Vector Method Summary-Cont

Type	Method Name	Description
		collection is null.
void	addElement (Object obj)	Adds the specified component to the end of this vector, increasing its size by one. The capacity of this vector is increased if its size becomes greater than its capacity. This method is identical in functionality to the add(Object) method (which is part of the List interface). Parameters: obj—the component to be added.
int	capacity ( )	Returns the current capacity of this vector. Returns: the current capacity (the length of its internal data array, kept in the field `elementData` of this vector).
void	clear ( )	Removes all of the elements from this Vector. The Vector will be empty after this call returns (unless it throws an exception). Specified by: clear in interface **List**

Object	clone ( )	Overrides: **clear** in class **AbstractList** Returns a clone of this vector. The copy will contain a reference to a clone of the internal data array, not a reference to the original internal data array of this `Vector` object. Overrides: **clone** in class **Object** Returns: a clone of this vector.
boolean	contains (Object elem)	Tests if the specified object is a component in this vector.
boolean	containsAll (Collection c)	Returns true if this Vector contains all of the elements in the specified Collection. Specified by: **contains** in interface **List** Overrides: **contains** in class **Abstract Collection**

Table 3. class Vector Method Summary-Cont

Type	Method Name	Description
		Parameters: c—an object. Returns: true if and only if the specified object is the same as a component in this vector, as determined by the equals method; false otherwise.

void	copyInto (Object [ ] anArray)	Copies the components of this vector into the specified array. The item at index k in this vector is copied into component k of anArray. The array must be big enough to hold all the objects in this vector, else an Index Out Of Bounds Exception is thrown. Parameters: `anArray`—the array into which the components get copied. Throws: **NullPointerException**—if the given array is null.
Object	elementAt (int index)	Returns the component at the specified index. This method is identical in functionality to the get method (which is part of the List interface). Parameters: `index`—an index into this vector. Returns: the component at the specified index. Throws: —**Array Index Out Of Bounds Exception**—if the `index` is negative or not less than the current size of this `Vector` object. given.
Enumeration	elements ( )	Returns an enumeration of the components of this vector. The returned `Enumeration` object will generate all items in this vector. The first item generated

is the item at index 0, then the
item at index 1, and so on.

Table 3. class Vector Method Summary-Cont

Type	Method Name	Description
		Returns: an enumeration of the components of this vector.
void	ensureCapacity (int minCapacity)	Increases the capacity of this vector, if necessary, to ensure that it can hold at least the number of components specified by the minimum capacity argument. If the current capacity of this vector is less than minCapacity, then its capacity is increased by replacing its internal data array, kept in the field elementData, with a larger one. The size of the new data array will be the old size plus capacityIncrement, unless the value of capacityIncrement is less than or equal to zero, in which case the new capacity will be twice the old capacity; but if this new size is still smaller than minCapacity, then the new capacity will be minCapacity. Parameters: minCapacity—the desired minimum capacity.
boolean	equals (Object o)	Compares the specified Object with this Vector for equality. Returns true if and only if the specified Object is also a List, both Lists have the same size,

and all corresponding pairs of elements in the two Lists are *equal*. (Two elements e1 and e2 are *equal* if (e1==null ? e2==null : e1.equals(e2)).) In other words, two Lists are defined to be equal if they contain the same elements in the same order.
Specified by:
equals in interface **List**
Overrides:
equals in class **AbstractList**
Parameters:
o—the Object to be compared for equality with this Vector.
Returns:
true if the specified Object is equal to this Vector

Table 3. class Vector Method Summary-Cont

Type	Method Name	Description
Object	firstElement ( )	Returns the first component (the item at index 0) of this vector. Returns: the first component of this vector. Throws: **No Such Element Exception**—if this vector has no components.
Object	get (int index)	Returns the element at the specified position in this Vector. Specified by: **get** in interface **List** Specified by: **get** in class **AbstractList** Parameters:

		index—index of element to return.
		Returns:
		object at the specified index
		Throws:
		Array Index Out Of Bounds Exception—index is out of range (index < 0 || index >= size( )).
int	hashCode ( )	Returns the hash code value for this Vector.
		Specified by:
		hashCode in interface **List**
		Overrides:
		hashCode in class **AbstractList**
		Returns:
		the hash code value for this list.
int	indexOf (Object elem)	Searches for the first occurence of the given argument, testing for equality using the equals method.
		Specified by:
		indexOf in interface **List**
		Overrides:
		indexOf in class **AbstractList**
		Parameters:
		elem—an object.
		Returns:
		the index of the first occurrence of the argument in this vector, that is, the smallest value k such that elem.equals(elementData[k])

Table 3. class Vector Method Summary-Cont

Type	Method Name	Description
		is true; returns—1 if the object is not found.
int	indexOf (Object elem, int index)	Searches for the first occurence of the given argument, beginning the search at index, and testing for equality using the equals method.
		Parameters:
		elem—an object.
		index—the non-negative index to start searching from.
		Returns:
		the index of the first occurrence of the object argument in this vector at position index or later in the vector, that is, the smallest value k such that elem.equals(elementData[k]) && (k >= index) is true; returns -1 if the object is not found. (Returns -1 if index >= the current size of this Vector.)
		Throws:
		Index Out Of Bounds Exception—if index is negative.
void	insertElementAt (Object obj, int index)	Inserts the specified object as a component in this vector at the specified index. Each component in this vector with an index greater or equal to the specified index is shifted upward to have an index one greater than

the value it had previously. The index must be a value greater than or equal to 0 and less than or equal to the current size of the vector. (If the index is equal to the current size of the vector, the new element is appended to the Vector.) This method is identical in functionality to the add(Object, int) method (which is part of the List interface). Note that the add method reverses the order of the parameters, to more closely match array usage.

Parameters:

obj—the component to insert.

index—where to insert the new component.

Table 3. class Vector Method Summary-Cont

Type	Method Name	Description
		Throws: **Array Index Out Of Bounds Exception**—if the index was invalid.
boolean	is Empty ( )	Tests if this vector has no components. Specified by: **is Empty** in interface **List** Overrides: **is Empty** in class **Abstract Collection** Returns: true if and only if this vector has no components, that is, its size is zero; false otherwise.

Object	lastElement ( )	Returns the last component of the vector. Returns: the last component of the vector, i.e., the component at index size( ) - 1. Throws: **NoSuchElementException**—if this vector is empty.
int	lastIndexOf (Object elem)	Returns the index of the last occurrence of the specified object in this vector. Specified by: **lastIndexOf** in interface **List** Overrides: **lastIndex Of** in class **AbstractList** Parameters: elem—the desired component. Returns: the index of the last occurrence of the specified object in this vector, that is, the largest value k such that elem. equals(elementData[k]) is true;returns -1 if the object is not found.
int	lastIndexOf (Object elem, int index)	Searches backwards for the specified object, starting from the specified index, and returns an index to it. Parameters: elem—the desired component. index—the index to start searching from.

Table 3. class Vector Method Summary-Cont

Type	Method Name	Description
		Returns: the index of the last occurrence of the specified object in this vector at position less than or equal to index in the vector, that is, the largest value k such that elem.equals(elementData[k]) && (k <= index) is true; -1 if the object is not found. (Returns -1 if index is negative.) Throws: **Index Out Of Bounds Exception**—if index is greater than or equal to the current size of this vector.
Object	remove (int index)	Removes the element at the specified position in this Vector. Shifts any subsequent elements to the left (subtracts one from their indices). Returns the element that was removed from the Vector. Specified by: **remove** in interface **List** Overrides: **remove** in class **AbstractList** Parameters: index—the index of the element to removed. Returns: element that was removed Throws:

| boolean | remove (Object o) | **Array Index Out Of Bounds Exception**—index out of range (index < 0 \|\| index >= size( )). Removes the first occurrence of the specified element in this Vector If the Vector does not contain the element, it is unchanged. More formally, removes the element with the lowest index i such that (o==null ? get(i)== null: o.equals(get(i))) (if such an element exists). Specified by: **remove** in interface **List** Overrides: **remove** in class **AbstractCollection** Parameters: o—element to be removed from this Vector, if present. |

Table 3. class Vector Method Summary-Cont

Type	**Method Name**	**Description**
		Returns: true if the Vector contained the specified element.
boolean	removeAll (Collection c)	Removes from this Vector all of its elements that are contained in the specified Collection. Specified by: **removeAll** in interface **List** Overrides: **removeAll** in class **Abstract Collection** Parameters:

		c—a collection of elements to be removed from the Vector Returns: true if this Vector changed as a result of the call. Throws: **NullPointerException**—if the specified collection is null.
void	removeAllElements( )	Removes all components from this vector and sets its size to zero. This method is identical in functionality to the clear method (which is part of the List interface).
boolean	removeElement (Object obj)	Removes the first (lowest-indexed) occurrence of the argument from this vector. If the object is found in this vector, each component in the vector with an index greater or equal to the object's index is shifted downward to have an index one smaller than the value it had previously. This method is identical in functionality to the remove Object) method (which is part of the List interface). Parameters: obj—the component to be removed. Returns: true if the argument was a component of this vector; false otherwise.

Table 3. class Vector Method Summary-Cont

Type	Method Name	Description
void	removeElementAt (int index)	Deletes the component at the specified index. Each component in this vector with an index greater or equal to the specified index is shifted downward to have an index one smaller than the value it had previously. The size of this vector is decreased by 1. The index must be a value greater than or equal to 0 and less than the current size of the vector. This method is identical in functionality to the remove method (which is part of the List interface). Note that the remove method returns the old value that was stored at the specified position. Parameters: index—the index of the object to remove. Throws: **Array Index Out Of Bounds Exception** —if the index was invalid.
protected	void removeRange (int fromIndex, int toIndex)	Removes from this List all of the elements whose index is between fromIndex, inclusive and toIndex, exclusive. This call shortens the ArrayList by (toIndex—fromIndex) elements. (If toIndex==fromIndex, this operation has no effect.)

		Overrides: **remove Range** in class **Abstract List** Parameters: `fromIndex`—index of first element to be removed. `toIndex`—index after last element to be removed.
boolean	retainAll (Collection c)	Retains only the elements in this Vector that are contained in the specified Collection. In other words, removes from this Vector all of its elements that are not contained in the specified Collection. Specified by: **retainAll** in interface **List**

Table 3. class Vector Method Summary-Cont

Type	Method Name	Description
		Overrides: **retainAll** in class **Abstract Collection** Parameters: `c`—a collection of elements to be retained in this Vector (all other elements are removed) Returns: true if this Vector changed as a result of the call. Throws: **NullPointerException**—if the specified collection is null.

Object	set (int index, Object element)	Replaces the element at the specified position in this Vector with the specified element.
void	setElementAt (Object obj, int index)	Sets the component at the specified index of this vector to be the specified object. The previous component at that position is discarded. The index must be a value greater than or equal to 0 and less than the current size of the vector. This method is identical in functionality to the set method (which is part of the List interface). Note that the set method reverses the order of the parameters, to more closely match array usage. Note also that the set method returns the old value that was stored at the specified position. Parameters: obj—what the component is to be set to. index—the specified index. Throws: **Array Index Out Of Bounds Exception**—if the index was invalid.
void	setSize (int newSize)	Sets the size of this vector. If the new size is greater than the current size, new null

Table 3. class Vector Method Summary-Cont

Type	Method Name	Description
		items are added to the end of the vector. If the new size is less than the current size, all components at index `newSize` and greater are discarded. Parameters: `newSize`—the new size of this vector. Throws: **Array Index Out Of Bounds Exception**—if new size is negative.
int	size ( )	Returns the number of components in this vector. Specified by: **size** in interface **List** Specified by: **size** in class **AbstractCollection** Returns: the number of components in this vector.
List	subList (int fromIndex, int toIndex)	Returns a view of the portion of this List between fromIndex, inclusive, and toIndex, exclusive. (If fromIndex and ToIndex are equal, the returned List is empty.) The returned List is backed by this List, so changes in the returned List are reflected in this List, and vice-versa. The returned List supports all of the optional List operations

supported by this List. This method eliminates the need for explicit range operations (of the sort that commonly exist for arrays). Any operation that expects a List can be used as a range operation by operating on a subList view instead of a whole List. For example, the following idiom removes a range of elements from a List: list.subList(from,to).clear( ); Similar idioms may be constructed for indexOf and lastIndexOf, and all of the algorithms in theCollections class can be applied to a subList.

Table 3. class Vector Method Summary-Cont

Type	Method Name	Description

The semantics of the List returned by this method become undefined if the backing list (i.e., this List) is *structurally modified* in any way other than via the returned List. (Structural modifications are those that change the size of the List, or otherwise perturb it in such a fashion that iterations in progress may yield incorrect results.)
Specified by:
subList in interface **List**
Overrides:
subList in class **AbstractList**
Parameters:
fromIndex—low endpoint

(inclusive) of the subList. `toIndex`—high endpoint (exclusive) of the subList.

Returns:

a view of the specified range within this List.

Throws:

Index Out Of Bounds Exception—endpoint index value out of range (`fromIndex < 0 || toIndex > size`)

Illegal Argument Exception—endpoint indices out of order (`fromIndex > toIndex`)

Object[]	toArray ( )	Returns an array containing all of the elements in this Vector in the correct order.

Specified by:

toArray in interface **List**

Overrides:

toArray in class **AbstractCollection**

Returns:

an array containing all of the elements in this collection.

Object [ ]	toArray (Object [ ] a)	Returns an array containing all of the elements in this Vector in the correct order; the runtime type of the returned array is that of the specified array. If the Vector fits in the specified array, it is returned therein.

Otherwise, a new array is allocated with the

Table 3. class Vector Method Summary-Cont

Type	Method Name	Description

---

runtime type of the specified array and the size of this Vector. If the Vector fits in the specified array with room to spare (i.e., the array has more elements than the Vector), the element in the array immediately following the end of the Vector is set to null. This is useful in determining the length of the Vector only if the caller knows that the Vector does not contain any null elements.

Specified by:

toArray in interface **List**

Overrides:

toArray in class **Abstract Collection**

Parameters:

a—the array into which the elements of the Vector are to be stored, if it is big enough; otherwise, a new array of the same runtime type is allocated for this purpose.

Returns:

an array containing the elements of the Vector.

Throws:

ArrayStoreException—the runtime type of a is not a supertype of the runtime type of every element in this Vector.

NullPointerException—if the given array is null.

String	toString ( )	Returns a string representation of this Vector, containing the String representation of each element. Overrides: **toString** in class **Abstract Collection** Returns: a string representation of this collection.
void	trimToSize ( )	Trims the capacity of this vector to be the vector's current size. If the capacity of this vector is larger than its current size, then the capacity is changed to equal the size by replacing its internal data array, kept in the field elementData, with a

Table 3. class Vector Method Summary-Cont

Type	Method Name	Description
		smaller one. An application can use this operation to minimize the storage of a vector.

Note: This is a modification of selected information from [14].

Appendix D
Selected HTML Tutorial

Hyper Text Markup Language (HTML) has productions or statements that are interpreted by browsers to render defined context. An HTML file is a text file containing small markup tags that direct the browser to display each page. An HTML file must have an htm or html file extension to direct the browser interpretation of the file. An HTML file can be created using a simple text editor or any editor with capability to save the output file in text format.

Open a text editor and type in the text in Figure D1.

```
<html>
<head>
<title>Title of page</title>
</head>
<body>
This is my first homepage. <b>This text is bold</b>
</body>
</html>
```
Figure D1. HTML First Page

Save the file as fpage.htm. Start your Internet browser. Select Open in the File menu of your browser. A dialog box will appear. Select Browse and locate the HTML file you just created called fpage.htm. Select the file and click Open. The address appears in the dialog box, for example C:\MyDocuments\fpage.htm. Click OK, and the browser will display the page.

The browser starts interpreting the tags in the open file fpage.htm. The page opens with the tag <html>. This tag tells your browser that this is the start of an HTML document. The last tag in your document is </html>. This tag tells your browser that this is the end of the HTML document.

The text between the <head> tag and the </head> tag is header information. Header information is not displayed in the browser window.

The text between the <title> tags is the title of your document. The title is displayed in your browser's caption.

The text between the <body> and </body> tags is the text that will be displayed in your browser.

The text between the <b> and </b> tags will be displayed in a bold font.

Most operating systems are installed with a HTML browser. The browser caches pages to avoid reading the same page twice. When you have changed a page, the browser must be notified to read the current copy of the open page. Use the browser's refresh/reload button located under the View menu item to force the browser to read the current open page.

D1. HTML Elements

HTML documents are text files made up of HTML elements defined using HTML tags.
HTML tags are surrounded by the two characters called angle brackets < and > used to mark-up HTML elements. HTML tags normally come in pairs like <b> and </b>. The first tag of an element content is the start tag. The tag that ends the element content is the same as the first with a forward slash following the open angle bracket of the end tag. HTML tags are not case sensitive, <b> means the same as <B>. In Figure D1, the text <b>This text is bold</b> is an HTML element. Also,

<body>
This is my first homepage. <b>This text is bold</b>
</body>
This is an HTML element that starts with <body> and ends with </body>.

The next generation of browsers may be lower case. The World Wide Web Consortium (W3C) recommends lowercase tags in their HTML 4 recommendation, and the next generation HTML (XHTML) demands lowercase tags.

D2. Tag Attributes

Tags can have attributes. Attributes provide additional information about HTML elements. The body of the HTML page in Figure D1 is opened or started with the tag <body>. One or more attributes may be added to the start tag, for example <body bycolor = "red">, tell the browser that the background color of the page should be red.

Attributes always come in name/value pairs. The color attribute in the body tag for a background color of red is bycolor = "red". The attribute name is bycolor and the value is "red". Attributes are always added to the start tag of an HTML element. Attribute values should always be enclosed in quotes. Double style quotes are the most common, but single style quotes are also allowed. When the attribute value itself contains quotes, it is necessary to use single quotes.

D2.1. Basic HTML Tags

The most important tags in HTML are tags that define headings, paragraphs and line breaks. The paragraph tag is <p> . . .</p>. The line break tag is a start only <br> for one line feed carriage return or advance to the next line of the page.

D2.2. Headings

Headings are defined with the <h1> to <h6> tags. <h1> defines the largest heading. <h6> defines the smallest heading.

```
<h1>This is a heading</h1>
<h2>This is a heading</h2>
<h3>This is a heading</h3>
<h4>This is a heading</h4>
<h5>This is a heading</h5>
<h6>This is a heading</h6>
```

HTML automatically adds an extra blank line before and after a heading.

D2.3. Paragraphs

Paragraphs are defined with the <p> tag.

```
<p>This is a paragraph</p>
```

HTML automatically adds an extra blank line before and after a paragraph.

D2.4. Line Breaks

The <br> tag is used when you want to end a line. The <br> tag forces a line break wherever you place it. The <br> tag is an empty tag with no closing tag.

This is my page.

D2.5. Comments in HTML

The comment tag is used to insert a comment in the HTML source code. A comment will be ignored by the browser and will not be seen while viewing the page. Comments can be used to explain your code.

<!-- This is a comment -->

An exclamation point is required after the opening bracket, but not before the closing bracket.

D2.6. Basic HTML Tags Summary

Tag	Description
<html>	Defines an HTML document
<body>	Defines the document's body
<h1> to <h6>	Defines header 1 to header 6
<p>	Defines a paragraph
 	Inserts a single line break
<hr>	Defines a horizontal rule
<!-->	Defines a comment

D3. HTML Text Formatting

Figure D2 details the use of selected HTML tags. Change the tags, save the current file content, open the page or refresh the page in the browser. Repeat this process until you understand the code.

<html>

```
<head>
<title>HTML Tags Summary</title>
</head>
<body>
<!—Selected HTML code page -->
<h3>Test a Few HTML Codes</h3>
<p>A paragraph tag is important in preparing text.<br>The next line in this
paragraph is Included in this text. The end of the paragraph. </p><b>This line
is bold.</b><br>
<hr>Draw a horizontal line.</hr>
</body>
</html>
```
Figure D2. HTML Tag Summary Page

D3.1. How to View HTML Source?

A Web page may be viewed if the implementer set controls on the server for viewing. To find out, click the VIEW option in your browser's toolbar and select SOURCE or PAGE SOURCE. This will open a window that displays the HTML code of the page.

D3.2. Text Formatting Tags Summary

Use the HTML page in Figure D2 and insert lines using the text formatting tags. Repeat this process one or two tags at-a-time, viewing the current HTML file after each tag insertion into the file.

Tag	Description
<b>	Defines bold text
<big>	Defines big text
<em>	Defines emphasized text
<i>	Defines italic text
<small>	Defines small text
<strong>	Defines strong text
<sub>	Defines subscripted text
<sup>	Defines superscripted text
<ins>	Defines inserted text
<del>	Defines deleted text
<s>	Deprecated. Use <del> instead

| <strike> | Deprecated. Use <del> instead |
| <u> | Deprecated. Use styles instead |

Computer Output Tags

Tag	Description
<code>	Defines computer code text
<kbd>	Defines keyboard text
<samp>	Defines sample computer code
<tt>	Defines teletype text
<var>	Defines a variable
<pre>	Defines preformatted text
<listing>	Deprecated. Use <pre> instead
<plaintext>	Deprecated. Use <pre> instead
<xmp>	Deprecated. Use <pre> instead

Citations, Quotations, and Definition Tags

Tag	Description
<abbr>	Defines an abbreviation
<acronym>	Defines an acronym
<address>	Defines an address element
<bdo>	Defines the text direction
<blockquote>	Defines a long quotation
<q>	Defines a short quotation
<cite>	Defines a citation
<dfn>	Defines a definition term

D4. HTML Character Entities

Some characters like the < character, have a special meaning in HTML, and therefore cannot be used in the text. To display a less than sign (<) in HTML, we have to use a character entity.

D4.1. Character Entities Summary

Some characters have a special meaning in HTML, like the less than sign (<) that defines the start of an HTML tag. If we want the browser to actually display these characters we must insert character entities in the HTML source.

A character entity has three parts: an ampersand (&), an entity name or a # and an entity number, and finally a semicolon (;).

To display a less than sign in an HTML document we must write: < or <

The advantage of using a name instead of a number is that a name is easier to remember. The disadvantage is that not all browsers support the newest entity names, while the support for entity numbers is very good in almost all browsers. Entities are case sensitive.

The Most Common Character Entities:

Result	Description	Entity Name	Entity Number
non-breaking	space		
<	less than	&lt;	&#60;
>	greater than	&gt;	&#62;
&	ampersand	&amp;	&#38;
"	quotation mark	&quot;	&#34;
'	apostrophe	&apos;	&#39;

Some Other Commonly Used Character Entities:

Result	Description	Entity Name	Entity Number
¢	cent	&cent;	&#162;
£	pound	&pound;	&#163;
¥	yen	&yen;	&#165;
§	section	&sect;	&#167;
©	copyright	&copy;	&#169;
®	registered trademark	&reg;	&#174;
×	multiplication	&times;	&#215;
÷	division	&divide;	&#247;

D5. HTML Links

HTML uses a hyperlink to link to another document on the Web.

D5.1. The Anchor Tag and the Href Attribute

HTML uses the <a> (anchor) tag to create a link to another document. An anchor can point to any resource on the Web: an HTML page, an image, a sound file, or a movie.

The syntax of creating an anchor:

<a href = "url">Text to be displayed</a>

The <a> tag is used to create an anchor to link from, the href attribute is used to address the document to link to, and the words between the open and close of the anchor tag will be displayed as a hyperlink.

D6. HTML Tables

D6.1. Tables

Tables are defined with the <table> tag. A table is divided into rows with the <tr> tag, and each row is divided into data cells with the <td> tag. The letters td stands for "table data," which is the content of a data cell. A data cell can contain text, images, lists, paragraphs, forms, horizontal rules, or tables. Figure D3 details selected HTML tags use in tables.

```
<html>
<body>
<table border="1">
<tr>
<td>row 1, cell 1</td>
<td>row 1, cell 2</td>
</tr>
<tr>
<td>row 2, cell 1</td>
<td>row 2, cell 2</td>
</tr>
</table>
```

```
</body>
</html>
```
Figure D3. Selected HTML Table Tags

Display the HTML page detailed in Figure D3 in your browser.

D6.1.1. Tables and the Border Attribute

If you do not specify a border attribute the table will be displayed without any borders. To display a table with borders, use the border attribute:

```
<html>
<body>
<table border="1">
<tr>
<td>Row 1, cell 1</td>
<td>Row 1, cell 2</td>
</tr>
</table>
</body>
</html>
```

D6.1.2. Headings in a Table

Headings in a table are defined with the <th> tag. View the HTML page in Figure D4 in a browser.

```
<html>
<body>
<table border="1">
<tr>
<th>Heading</th>
<th>Another Heading</th>
</tr>
<tr>
<td>row 1, cell 1</td>
<td>row 1, cell 2</td>
</tr>
<tr>
<td>row 2, cell 1</td>
```

```
<td>row 2, cell 2</td>
</tr>
</table>
</body>
</html>
```
Figure D4. HTML Table Heading Tag

Blank space or empty data cells with a non-breaking space use the character entity   in Figure D5:

```
<html>
<body>
<table border="1">
<tr>
<td>row 1, cell 1</td>
<td>row 1, cell 2</td>
</tr>
<tr>
<td>row 2, cell 1</td>
<td> </td>
</tr>
</table>
</body>
</html>
```
Figure D5. Character Entity

D6.1.3. Table Tags Summary

Tag	Description
<table>	Defines a table
<th>	Defines a table header
<tr>	Defines a table row
<td>	Defines a table cell
<caption>	Defines a table caption
<colgroup>	Defines groups of table columns
<col>	Defines the attribute values for one or more columns in a table
<thead>	Defines a table head

<tbody>   Defines a table body
<tfoot>   Defines a table footer

D7. HTML Lists

HTML supports ordered, unordered and definition lists.

D7.1. Unordered Lists

An unordered list is a list of items. The list items are marked with bullets. An unordered list starts with the <ul> tag. Each list item starts with the <li> tag. Open the browser with the page detailed in Figure D6.

```
<html>
<body>
<ul>
<li>Coffee</li>
<li>Milk</li>
</ul>
</body>
</html>
```
Figure D6. Unordered List

D7.2. Ordered Lists

An ordered list is also a list of items. The list items are marked with numbers. An ordered list starts with the <ol> tag. Each list item starts with the <li> tag. Open the browser with the page detailed in Figure D7.

```
<html>
<body>
<ol>
<li>Coffee</li>
<li>Milk</li>
</ol>
</body>
</html>
```
Figure D7. Ordered List

D7.3. List Tags Summary

Tag	Description
<ol>	Defines an ordered list
<ul>	Defines an unordered list
<li>	Defines a list item
<dl>	Defines a definition list
<dt>	Defines a definition term
<dd>	Defines a definition description
<dir>	Deprecated. Use <ul> instead
<menu>	Deprecated. Use <ul> instead

D8. HTML Forms and Input

HTML Forms are used to select different kinds of user input.

D8.1. Forms

A form is an area that can contain form elements. Form elements are elements that allow the user to enter information like text fields, textarea fields, drop-down menus, radio buttons, and checkboxes in a form.

A form is defined with the <form> tag.

```
<form>
 <input>
 <input>
</form>
```

D8.2. Input

The form tag <input> receives input specified with the type attribute. Selected input types are text, radio, and checkbox.

D8.3. Text Fields

Text fields in Figure D8 are used when you want the user to type letters and numbers in a form.

```
<html>
```

```
<body>
<form>
First name:
<input type="text" name="firstname">
<br>
</form>
</body>
</html>
```
Figure D8. Form With Text Fields

D8.4. Radio Buttons

Radio Buttons in Figure D9 are used when you want the user to select one of a limited number of choices.

```
<html>
<body>
<form>
<input type="radio" name="sex" value="male"> Male
<br>
<input type="radio" name="sex" value="female"> Female
</form>
</body>
</html>
```
Figure D9. Form Radio Buttons

D8.5. Checkboxes

Checkboxes in Figure D10 are used when you want the user to select one or more options of a limited number of choices.

```
<html>
<body>
<form>
<input type="checkbox" name="bike">
I have a bike
<br>
<input type="checkbox" name="car">
I have a car
</form>
```

```
</body>
</html>
```
Figure D10. Form Checkboxes

D8.6. The Form's Action Attribute and the Submit Button

When the user clicks on the "Submit" button, the content of the form is sent to another file. The form's action attribute in Figure 11 defines the name of the code to act on the form content data.

```
<html>
<body>
<form name="input" action="form_action.php"
method="get">
Username:
<input type="text" name="user">
<input type="submit" value="Submit">
</form>
</html>
</body>
```
Figure D11. Form Action Attribute

If you type some characters in the text field, and click the "Submit" button, you will send your input to an area where the action code called form_action.php take action defined in the code. The action code parses the data with commands defined by the user.

D8.7. Form Tags Summary

Tag	Description
<form>	Defines a form for user input
<input>	Defines an input field
<textarea>	Defines a text-area (a multi-line text input control)
<label>	Defines a label to a control
<fieldset>	Defines a fieldset
<legend>	Defines a caption for a fieldset
<select>	Defines a selectable list (a drop-down box)
<optgroup>	Defines an option group
<option>	Defines an option in the drop-down box

| `<button>` | Defines a push button |
| `<isindex>` | Deprecated. Use `<input>` instead |

D9. HTML Images

With HTML you can display images in a document.

D9.1. The Image Tag and the Src Attribute

In HTML, images are defined with the `<img>` tag. The `<img>` tag is empty, which means that it contains attributes only and it has no closing tag. To display an image on a page, you need to use the src attribute. Src stands for "source". The value of the src attribute is the URL of the image you want to display on your page.

The syntax of defining an image:

`<img src="url">`

The URL points to the location where the image is stored. An image named "vally. gif" located in the directory "images" on "www.50megs.com" has the URL: http:// www.50megs.com/images/vally.gif.

The browser puts the image where the image tag occurs in the document. If you put an image tag between two paragraphs, the browser displays the first paragraph, then the image, and then the second paragraph.

D9.2. The Alt Attribute

The alt attribute is used to define an "alternate text" for an image. The value of the alt attribute is an author-defined text:

`<img src="vally.gif" alt="Travel">`

The "alt" attribute tells the reader what he or she is missing on a page if the browser can't load images. The browser will then display the alternate text instead of the image. It is a good practice to include the "alt" attribute for each image on a page, to improve the display and usefulness of your document for people who have text-only browsers.

D9.3. Image Tags Summary

Tag	Description
<img>	Defines an image
<map>	Defines an image map
<area>	Defines a clickable area inside an image map

Note: This is a modification of selected information from [13, 15].

Appendix E
Selected PHP Tutorial

Hypertext Preprocessor (PHP) is a server-side scripting language. PHP scripts are executed on the server. The PHP supports many databases such as MySQL, Informix, Oracle, Sybase, Solid, PostgreSQL, and Generic ODBC. PHP is an open source software (OSS) that is free to download and use. Hypertext Preprocessor files may contain text, HTML tags, and scripts. PHP files are returned to the browser as plain HTML. Valid file extensions are ".php", ".php3", or ".phtml".

MySQL is a database server. It is ideal for both small and large applications. The MySQL database engine supports Standard Query Language (SQL). The relational database system is implemented on a number of platforms. MySQL is free to download and use. PHP combined with MySQL are cross-platform and supports development in Windows, UNIX, and Linux server platforms.

This scripting language translator runs on different platforms such as Windows, Linux, and UNIX. PHP is compatible with almost all servers used today, for example Apache and Information Interchange Server (IIS). An official resource free PHP can be downloaded from the web site www.php.net. PHP is easy to learn and runs efficiently on the server side of networks.

I recommend the Apache server to implement applications that are compatible under several operating systems. The Linux and UNIX operating systems in many cases include the Apache server software. The Linux operating system files include PHP and MySQL. An install sequence to run PHP and MySQL with the Apache server is:

Install an Apache server on a Windows, Linux or UNIX machine.
Install PHP on a Windows, Linux or UNIX machine.
Install MySQL on a Windows, Linux, or UNIX machine.

This tutorial will not explain how to install PHP, MySQL, or Apache Server. The installation of these software programs is accomplished with a click on their install wizard or a well-defined set of steps. Users can configure their machines as servers and develop client and server side applications executing the browser on the localhost.

If your server supports PHP create some .php files in your web directory and the server will parse them for you through your browser. Most web hosts offer PHP support.

If your server does not support PHP, you must install PHP. A link to a tutorial from PHP.net to install PHP5 is http://www.php.net/manual/en/install.php. Download a free copy of PHP from http://www.php.net/downloads.php. Download a free copy of MySQL database software from http://www.mysql.com/downloads/index.html. Download a free copy of Apache Server from http://httpd.apache.org/.

E1. PHP Syntax

The server can be configured to block the view of the PHP source code by selecting "View source" in the browser. The HTML source code can be blocked from view by embedding the HTML in the PHP code. Generate the HTML code from the PHP script with the server configured to block PHP code viewing. In this case you will only see the output from the PHP file, which is plain HTML. PHP scripts are executed on the server before the result is sent back to the browser.

E2. Basic PHP Syntax

A PHP scripting code block always starts with <?php and ends with ?>. A PHP scripting block can be placed anywhere in the document. On servers with shorthand support enabled you can start a scripting block with <? and end with ?>. To insure maximum compatibility, use the <?php . . . ?> standard block.

A PHP file normally contains HTML tags, just like an HTML file, and some PHP scripting code enclosed in the PHP block format that is executed on the server.

Figure E1 is a simple PHP script which sends the text "My First PHP Script" to the browser:

```
<html>
<body><?php
echo "My First PHP Script";
```

?></body>
</html>
Figure E1. First PHP Program

Each script language PHP statement must end with a semicolon. The semicolon is a separator and is used to distinguish one set of instructions from another. The C Programming Language and Java Programming Language statements end with a semicolon.

Two basic statements output text with PHP are echo and print. Figure E1 details the use of the echo statement to output the text "My First PHP Script".

E2.1. Comments in PHP

In PHP, // is used to make a single-line comment or /* and */ to make a large comment block. The C and Java Programming Languages use the same comment format. A valid PHP comment is detailed in Figure E2.

<html>
<body><?php //This is a comment that end at the end of a single-line
/*
This is
a comment
block
*/ ?></body>
</html>
Figure E2. PHP Comment

E2.2. Variables in PHP

Variables are used for storing values, such as numbers, strings, or function results for use many times in a script. All variables in PHP start with a $ sign symbol. Variables may contain strings, numbers, or arrays.

In Figure E3, the PHP script assigns the string "My First PHP Script" to a variable called $txt:

<html>
<body><?php
$txt = "My First PHP Script";

```
echo $txt;
?></body>
</html>
```
Figure E3. PHP Variable Assignment

To concatenate two or more variables together, use the dot (.) operator:

```
<html>
<body><?php
$txt1 = "My First PHP Script";
$txt2 = "1234";
echo $txt1 . " " . $txt2 ;
?></body>
</html>
```
Figure E4. Concatenate Variables

The output of the script in Figure E4 will be: "My First PHP Script 1234".

E2.3. Variable Naming Rules

PHP variable naming rules are:
A variable name must start with a letter or an underscore "_"
A variable name can only contain alpha-numeric characters and underscores (a-Z, 0-9, and _)
A variable name should not contain spaces. If a variable name should be more than one word, it should be separated with underscore ($my_string), or with capitalization ($myString)

E2.4. PHP Operators

Operators are used to operate on values. Selected operators used in PHP are detailed in Figure E5 through Figure E8.

Operator	Description	Example	Result
+	Addition	x = 4 x + 2	6
-	Subtraction	x = 3 5 - x	2
*	Multiplication	x = 4 x * 5	20
/	Division	15 / 5 5/2	3 2.5
%	Modulus	5 % 2 10 % 8	1 2
++	Increment	x = 5 x++	x = 6

| -- | Decrement | x = 5 x-- | x = 4 |

Figure E5. Arithmetic Operators

Operator	Example Is	The Same As
=	x = y	x = y
+=	x += y	x = x + y
-=	x -= y	x = x - y
*=	x *= y	x = x * y
/=	x /= y	x = x / y
%=	x %= y	x = x % y

Figure E6. Assignment Operators

Operator	Description	Example
==	is equal to	5 == 8 returns false
!=	is not equal	5 != 8 returns true
>	is greater than	5 > 8 returns false
<	is less than	5 < 8 returns true
>=	is greater than or equal to	5 >= 8 returns false
<=	is less than or equal to	5 <= 8 returns true

Figure E7. Comparison Operators

Operator	Description	Example
&&	and x = 6 y = 3	(x < 10 && y > 1) returns true
||	or x = 6 y = 3	(x == 5 || y == 5) returns false
!	not x = 6 y = 3	!(x == y) returns true

Figure E8. Logical Operators

E2.5. PHP If ... Else Statements

E2.5.1. The If ... Else Statement

Execute one set of code for a true if condition and another set of code for a false if condition with an if....else statement.

Syntax
if (condition)
   code to be executed if condition is true;

else
  code to be executed if condition is false;

The script in Figure D9 will output "The Sun is up!" if the current day is Friday, otherwise it will output "The Sun is down!":

```
<html>
<body><?php
$d = date("D");
if ($d == "Fri")
  echo "The Sun is up!";
else
  echo "The Sun is down!";
?></body>
</html>
```
Figure E9. if ... else Statement

A script with multiple statements in the scope of an if-statement is detailed in Figure E10. The statements should be enclosed within curly braces.

```
<html>
<body><?php
$d = date("D");
if ($d == "Fri")
  {
  echo "Today!<br />";
  echo "The Sun is up!";
  echo "See you on Monday!";
  }
?></body>
</html>
```
Figure E10. if Statement with Multiple Statements in the Scope

E2.6. The ElseIf Statement

If you want to execute some code if one of several conditions is true use the elseif statement

Syntax
if (condition)
  code to be executed if condition is true;
elseif (condition)
  code to be executed if condition is true;
else
  code to be executed if condition is false;

Figure E11 details a script that output "Have a long trip!" if the current day is Friday, and "Have a nice Day!" if the current day is Sunday. Otherwise it will output "Have a short trip!":

```
<html>
<body><?php
$d = date("D");
if ($d == "Fri")
  echo "Have a long trip!";
elseif ($d == "Sun")
  echo "Have a nice day!";
else
  echo "Have a short trip!";
?></body>
</html>
```
Figure E11. Elseif Statement

E2.7. The Switch Statement

The Switch statement in PHP is used to perform one of several different actions based on one of several different conditions. If you want to select one of many blocks of code to be executed, use the Switch statement. The switch statement is used to avoid long blocks of if..elseif..else code.

Syntax
```
switch (expression)
{
case label1:
  code to be executed if expression = label1;
  break;
case label2:
  code to be executed if expression = label2;
```

```
  break;
default:
  code to be executed
  if expression is different
  from both label1 and label2;
}
```

A single expression is evaluated once. The value of the expression is compared with the values for each case in the structure. If there is a match, the code associated with that case is executed. After a code segment is executed, break is used to stop the code from running into the next case. The default statement is used if none of the cases are true. Figure E12 details a script using the case statement.

```
<html>
<body><?php
switch ($x)
{
case 1:
  echo "Number 1";
  break;
case 2:
  echo "Number 2";
  break;
case 3:
  echo "Number 3";
  break;
default:
  echo "No number between 1 and 3";
}
?></body>
</html>
```
Figure E12. Case Statement

E2.8. PHP Arrays

An array can store one or more values in a single variable name. Each element in the array has its own ID so that it can be easily accessed. There are three different kinds of arrays:

Numeric array - An array with a numeric ID key
Associative array - An array where each ID key is associated with a value
Multidimensional array - An array containing one or more arrays

Numeric Arrays

A numeric array stores each element with a numeric ID key. There are different ways to create a numeric array.

An array created in which the ID is automatically assigned:

$names = array("James","Matthew","John");

An array created in which the ID key is assigned manually:

$names [0] = "James";
$names [1] = "Matthew";
$names [2] = "John";

The ID keys in Figure E13 generate the output Matthew and John are James's neighbors.

```
<html>
<body>
<?php$names [0] = "James";
$names [1] = "Matthew";
$names [2] = "John";
echo $names [1] . "and" . $names [2] . "are". $names [0] . "'s neighbors";
?>
</body>
</html>
```
Figure E13. Array Manual Assigned IDs

E2.9. Associative Arrays

An associative array, each ID key is associated with a value. When storing data about specific named values, a numerical array is not always the best way to do it. With associative arrays we can use the values as keys and assign values to them.

Assign ages to the different persons.

```
$ages = array ("James"=>32, "Matthew"=>30, "John"=>34);
```

A different way of creating the array with different ages stored in the array.

```
$ages ['James'] = "32";
$ages ['Matthew'] = "30";
$ages ['John'] = "34";
```

The ID keys in Figure E14 generate the output James is 32 years old.

```
<html>
<body>
<?php$ages ['James'] = "32";
$ages ['Matthew'] = "30";
$ages ['John'] = "34";
echo "James is" . $ages ['James'] . "years old.";
?>
</body>
</html>
```
Figure E14. Associative Array Assigned IDs

E2.10. PHP Looping

Looping statements in PHP are used to execute the same block of code a specified number of times.

Looping
PHP looping statements are:

while—loops through a block of code if and as long as a specified program control condition is true; The test condition is at the beginning of the code block.
do...while—loops through a block of code once, and then repeats the loop as long as a special program control condition is true; The test condition is at the end of the code block.
for - loops through a block of code a specified number of times
foreach - loops through a block of code for each element in an array

E2.11. The while Statement

The while-statement executes a block of code as long as a control expression test condition is true.

Syntax
while (condition)
code to be executed;

Figure E15 details a loop that will continue to run as long as the control variable i is less than, or equal to 5. The control variable i will increase by 1 each time the loop runs.

```
<html>
<body>
<?php
$i = 1;
while($i <= 5)
  {
    echo "The number is" . $i . "<br />";
    $i++;
  }
?>
</body>
</html>
```
Figure E15. while Loop

E2.12. The do...while Statement

The do ... while statement will execute a block of code at least once. The execution will repeat the loop as long as a control expression condition is true.

Syntax
do
{
code to be executed;
}
while (condition);

The script in Figure E16 will increment the value of i at least once, and it will continue incrementing the variable i as long as it has a value of less than 5:

```
<html>
<body><?php
$i=0;
do
  {
    $i++;
    echo "The number is" . $i . "<br />";
  }
while ($i < 5);
?></body>
</html>
```
Figure E16. do . . while Loop

E2.13. The for Statement

The for-statement is used when you the number of times you want to execute a statement or a list of statements.

```
Syntax
for (initialization; condition; increment)
{
  code to be executed;
}
```

The for-statement has three parameters. The first parameter initializes variables, the second parameter holds the condition, and the third parameter contains the increments required to implement the loop. If more than one variable is included in the initialization or the increment parameter, they should be separated by commas. The condition must evaluate to true or false.

The script in Figure E17 prints the text "My First PHP Script!" five times:

```
<html>
<body><?php
for ($i = 1; $i <= 5; $i++)
{
```

```
echo "My First PHP Script!<br />";
}
?></body>
</html>
```
Figure E17. for Loop

E2.14. The foreach Statement

The foreach statement is used to loop through arrays.

For every loop, the value of the current array element is assigned to $value and the array pointer is moved by one to access at the next element.

Syntax
```
foreach (array as value)
{
    code to be executed;
}
```

Figure E18 details a loop that will print the values of array.

```
<html>
<body><?php
$arr=array ("one", "two", "three"); foreach ($arr as $value)
{
  echo "Value:" . $value . "<br />";
}
?></body>
</html>
```
Figure E18. foreach Statement

E2.3. PHP Functions

A function is a block of code that can be executed whenever we need it. There are more than 700 built-in functions available in PHP. This tutorial emphasizes the syntax of user created functions.

E2.3.1. Create a PHP Function

PHP functions are created with attributes:

All functions start with the word function ( )
Name the function with a name that describes what the function does by its name.
The name starts with a letter or underscore.
Add a "{" to open the function code.
Insert the function code.
Add a "}" to close the function code.

The function called writeMyName in Figure E19 has two parameters and is called three times in the script.

```
<html>
<body><?php
// The name of this function is writeMyName
function writeMyName($fname,$punctuation)
{
  echo $fname . "Refsnes" . $punctuation . "<br />";
} // End writeMyName
echo "My name is ";
writeMyName ("Kai Jim", "."); echo "My name is";
writeMyName ("Hege", "!"); echo "My name is";
writeMyName ("Ståle", "...");
?></body>
</html>
```
Figure E19. Function with Parameters

The output of the code in Figure E19 is:

My name is Kai Jim Refsnes.
My name is Hege Refsnes!
My name is Ståle Refsnes...

E2.3.2. PHP Functions—Return values

The function in Figure E20 returns a value when it is called.

```
<html>
<body><?php
// Add two numbers and return the sum
```

```
function add ($x, $y)
{
  $total = $x + $y;
  return $total;
} // End add
echo "1 + 16 =" . add (1,16);
?></body>
</html>
```
Figure E20. Function Return Values

The output of the code in Figure 20 is 1 + 16 = 17.

E2.3.3. PHP Forms and User Input

The PHP $_GET and $_POST retrieves information from form variables. Form variables are defined in the form input tag attribute name.

E2.3.4. PHP Form Handling

Form elements in an HTML page are automatically available to PHP scripts.

```
<html>
<body><form action = "welcome.php" method = "post">
Name: <input type="text" name="name" />
Age: <input type="text" name="age" />
<input type="submit" />
</form></body>
</html>
```
Figure E21. HTML Page

Figure E21 details an HTML page that contains two input fields and a submit button. When the user fills in this form and click on the submit button, the form data is sent to an area that the form action code welcome.php is defined to parse the form data. The form action code is stored in a file with the name of the form action parameter. In PHP this code may be stored in the same file that contains the form. In this case, special script coding is used to manage the form data parsing.

The form action welcome.php is detailed in Figure E22.

```
<html>
```

```
<body>Welcome <?php echo $_POST [ "name" ]; ?>.<br />
You are <?php echo $_POST [ "age" ]; ?> years old.</body>
</html>
```
Figure E22. Form Action Code for welcome.php

Output for form input John to form variable name and 18 to form variable age is parsed by the form action code welcome.php in Figure E22.

Welcome John.
You are 28 years old.

The PHP $_GET and $_POST variables are explained in Section E2.4.

E2.3.5. Form Validation

User input should be validated on the browser whenever possible by client scripts such as JavaScript.

User input maybe validated using the server. One way to validate a form on the server is to post the form to itself, instead of jumping to a different page. The user will then get the error messages on the same page as the form. This makes it easier to discover the error. It is also easier for the developer to manage the error conditions under script control.

E2.4. PHP $_GET

E2.4.1. The $_GET Variable

Information about the $_GET variable is:

The $_GET variable is used to collect values from a form with method="get".
The $_GET variable is an array of variable names and values sent by the HTTP GET method.
The $_GET variable is used to collect values from a form with method="get". Information sent from a form with the GET method is visible to everyone displayed in the browser's address bar. A maximum of 100 characters maybe displayed in the browser's address bar.

The form code in Figure E23 details the use of $_GET.

```
<html>
<body>
<form action="welcome.php" method="get">
Name: <input type="text" name="name" />
Age: <input type="text" name="age" />
<input type="submit" />
</form>
</body>
</html>
```
Figure E23. $_GET HTML Form

The user inserts Henry for name and 24 for age in the form. The user clicks the "Submit" button. A URL sent could look something like this:

http://www3.50megs.com/welcome.php?name=Henry&age=24

The welcome.php file can now use the $_GET variable to parse the form data. The names of the form fields will automatically be the ID keys in the $_GET array:

```
Welcome <?php echo $_GET [ "name" ]; ?>.<br />
You are <?php echo $_GET [ "age" ]; ?> years old!
```

Some $_GET variable limits are:

All variable names and values are displayed in the URL. This method should not be used when sending passwords or other sensitive information.
The HTTP GET method is not suitable on large variable values; the value cannot exceed 100 characters.

E2.5. The $_REQUEST Variable

The PHP $_REQUEST variable contains the contents of both $_GET, $_POST, and $_COOKIE.

The PHP $_REQUEST variable can be used to get the result from form data sent with both the GET and POST methods.

Substitute $_REQUEST for $_POST in the form action code welcome.php in Figure E22 for the same result as $_POST:

Welcome <?php echo $_REQUEST["name"]; ?>.
You are <?php echo $_REQUEST["age"]; ?> years old!

E2.6. PHP $_POST

The $_POST variable is used to collect values from a form with method = "post".

E2.6.1. The $_POST Variable

The $_POST variable is an array of variable names and values sent by the HTTP POST method.

The $_POST variable is used to collect values from a form with method = "post". Information sent from a form with the POST method is invisible to others and has no limits on the amount of information to send. Figure E24 details a HTML form using $_POST.

```
<html>
<body>
<form action="welcome.php" method="post">
Enter your name: <input type="text" name="name" />
Enter your age: <input type="text" name="age" />
<input type="submit" />
</form>
</body>
</html>
```
Figure E24. HTML Form Using $_POST

When the user clicks the "Submit" button, the URL will not contain any form data, and will look something like this:

http://www3.50megs.com/welcome.php

The welcome.php file defined in Figure E22 can now use the $_POST variable to catch the form data. The names of the form fields are automatically the ID keys in the $_POST array:

Welcome <?php echo $_POST ["name"]; ?>.
You are <?php echo $_POST ["age"]; ?> years old!

A reason to use $_POST:

Variables sent with HTTP POST are not shown in the URL.
Variables have no length limit. However, because the variables are not displayed in the URL, it is not possible to bookmark the page.

The $_REQUEST Variable:

The PHP $_REQUEST variable contains the contents of both $_GET, $_POST, and $_COOKIE.
The PHP $_REQUEST variable can be used to get the result from form data sent with both the GET and POST methods:

Welcome <?php echo $_REQUEST["name"]; ?>.
You are <?php echo $_REQUEST["age"]; ?> years old!

E2.7. PHP Date ( )

The PHP date ( ) function is used to format a time or a date.

E2.7.1. The PHP Date ( ) Function

The PHP date ( ) function formats a timestamp to a more readable date and time.

Syntax
date (format,timestamp)

Parameter	Description
format Required.	Specifies the format of the timestamp.
timestamp Optional.	Specifies a timestamp. Default is the current date and time as a timestamp.

A timestamp is the number of seconds since January 1, 1970 at 00:00:00 GMT. This is also known as the Unix Timestamp.
PHP Date—Format the Date

The first parameter in the date ( ) function specifies how to format the date/time. It uses letters to represent date and time formats. Here are some of the letters that can be used:

d - The day of the month (01-31)
m - The current month, as a number (01-12)
Y - The current year in four digits
An overview of all the letters that can be used in the format parameter, can be found in our PHP Date reference.

Other characters, like"/", ".", or "-" can also be inserted between the letters to add additional formatting:

```
<html>
<body>
<?php
echo date("Y/m/d");
echo "<br />";
echo date("Y.m.d");
echo "<br />";
echo date("Y-m-d");
?>
</body>
<html>
```
Figure E25. PHP Date Formatting

The output of the code in Figure E25 could be something like this:

2006/07/11
2006.07.11
2006-07-11

E2.8. PHP File Handling

The fopen ( ) function is used to open files in PHP.

E2.8.1. Opening a File

The fopen ( ) function is used to open files in PHP.

The first parameter of this function contains the name of the file to be opened and the second parameter specifies in which mode the file should be opened:

```
<html>
<body><?php
$file=fopen ("welcome.txt", "r");
?></body>
</html>
```

The file may be opened in one of the following modes:

Modes Description

Modes		Description
r	Read only.	Starts at the beginning of the file
r+	Read/Write.	Starts at the beginning of the file
w	Write only.	Opens and clears the contents of file; or creates a new file if it doesn't exist
w+	Read/Write.	Opens and clears the contents of file; or creates a new file if it doesn't exist
a	Append.	Opens and writes to the end of the file or creates a new file if it doesn't exist
a+	Read/Append.	Preserves file content by writing to the end of the file
x	Write only.	Creates a new file. Returns FALSE and an error if file already exists
x+	Read/Write.	Creates a new file. Returns FALSE and an error if file already exists

Note: If the fopen ( ) function is unable to open the specified file, it returns 0 for false.

Figure E26 generates a message if the fopen ( ) function is unable to open the specified file:

```
<html>
<body><?php
$file=fopen ("welcome.txt", "r") or exit ("Unable to open file!"); ?>
</body>
</html>
```
Figure E26. fopen Open Failure

E2.8.2. Closing a File

The fclose ( ) function is used to close an open file:

```
<?php
$file = fopen ("test.txt", "r"); //some code to be executedfclose($file);
?>
```

E2.8.3. Check End-of-file

The feof ( ) function checks if the "end-of-file" (EOF) has been reached.

The feof ( ) function is useful for looping through data of unknown length.

You cannot read from files opened in w, a, and x mode.

```
if (feof ($file)) echo "End of file";
```

E2.8.4. Reading a File Line by Line

The fgets ( ) function is used to read a single line from a file. After a call to this function the file pointer has moved to the next line.

Figure E27 reads a file line by line, until the end of file is reached:

```
<html>
<body>
<?php
$file = fopen ("welcome.txt", "r") or exit ("Unable to open file!");
//Output a line of the file until the end is reached
while (!feof ($file))
{
    echo fgets ($file). "<br />";
}
fclose ($file);
?>
</body>
</html>
Figure E27. Read a File
```

E2.8.5. Reading a File Character by Character

The fgetc ( ) function is used to read a single character from a file. After a call to this function the file pointer moves to the next character.

Figure E28 reads a file character by character, until the end of file is reached:

```
<html>
<body>
<?php
$file=fopen ("welcome.txt", "r") or exit ("Unable to open file!");
while (!feof ($file))
  {
  echo fgetc ($file);
  }
fclose ($file);
?>
</body>
</html>
```
Figure E28. Reads a File Character by Character

E2.9. Connecting to a MySQL Database

Before you can access and work with data in a database, you must create a connection to the database. In PHP, a database connection is done with the mysql_connect ( ) function.

Syntax
mysql_connect (servername, username, password);

Parameter	Description
servername Optional.	Specifies the server to connect to. Default value is "localhost:3306"
username Optional.	Specifies the username to log in with. Default value is the name of the user that owns the server process
password Optional.	Specifies the password to log in with. Default is ""

Store the connection in a variable ($con) for later use in the script. The "die" part will be executed if the connection fails. A MySQL connection is detailed in Figure E29.

```
<html>
<body>
<?php
$con = mysql_connect ("localhost", "joe", "tqr496");
if (!$con)
{
   die ('Could not connect: ' . mysql_error ( ));
} // End if
?>
</body>
</html>
```
Figure 29. MySQL Connection

E2.10. Closing a Connection

The connection will be closed as soon as the script ends. To close the connection before the script ends use the mysql_close ( ) function. A MySQL connection is closed in Figure E30.

```
<html>
<body>
<?php
// Connect to MySQL
$con = mysql_connect ("localhost", "joe", "tqr496");
if (!$con)
   {
   die ('Could not connect: ' . mysql_error ( ));
   } // End if
// Other PHP statements
mysql_close ($con);
?>
</body>
</html>
```
Figure E30. MySQL Connection Close

E2.11. PHP MySQL Insert Into

The INSERT INT ( ) statement is used to insert new records into a database table.

E2.11.1. Insert Data into a Database Table

The INSERT INTO statement is used to add new records to a database table.

Syntax
INSERT INTO table_name
VALUES (value1, value2, …)

You can also specify the columns where you want to insert the data:

INSERT INTO table_name (column1, column2,…)
VALUES (value1, value2, …

Structured Query Language (SQL) statements are not case sensitive. INSERT INTO is the same as insert into. The mysql_query ( ) function is used to execute SQL statements in PHP.

The script in Figure E31 adds two new records to the Person table.

```
<html>
<body>
<?php
// Connect to MySQL
$con = mysql_connect ("localhost","joe","tqr496");
if (!$con)
{
  die('Could not connect: ' . mysql_error ( ));
} // End if
// Select the database my_db
mysql_select_db ("my_db", $con);
// Execute the SQL insert statement
mysql_query ("INSERT INTO person (FirstName, LastName, Age) VALUES ('James', 'Griffin', '35')");
mysql_query ("INSERT INTO person (FirstName, LastName, Age)
VALUES ('Glenn', 'Matthew', '33')");mysql_close ($con);
?>
</body>
</html>
```
Figure E31. Add Records to a MySQL Database

E2.12. Insert Data from a Form into a Database

Figure E32 creates an HTML form to add new records to the Person table.

```
<html>
<body><form action="insert.php" method="post">
Firstname: <input type="text" name="firstname" />
Lastname: <input type="text" name="lastname" />
Age: <input type="text" name="age" />
<input type="submit" />
</form></body>
</html>
```
Figure E32. An HTML Form

When a user clicks the submit button in the HTML form in Figure E32, the form data is sent to form action code insert.php. The insert.php file in Figure E33 connects to a database, and retrieves the values from the form with the PHP $_POST variables. Then, the mysql_query ( ) function executes the INSERT INTO statement, and a new record will be added to the database table.

```
<html>
<body>
<?php
// Connect to MySQL
$con = mysql_connect ("localhost", "joe", "tqr496");
if (!$con)
{
  die ('Could not connect: ' . mysql_error ( ));
} // End if
// Select a database my_db
mysql_select_db ("my_db", $con);
// Define an SQL insert statement string with the input form variables content
$sql="INSERT INTO person (FirstName, LastName, Age)
VALUES ('$_POST [ firstname ]','$_POST [ lastname ]','$_POST [ age ]')";
// Execute the SQL insert statement string
if (!mysql_query ($sql, $con))
{
  die ('Error: ' . mysql_error( ));
} // End if
```

```
echo "1 record added";
// Close the mysql connection
mysql_close ($con);
?>
</body>
</html>
```
Figure E33. Form Action Code for insert.php

E2.13. PHP MySQL Select

The SELECT statement is used to select data from a database.

E2.13.1. Select Data From a Database Table

The SELECT statement is used to select data from a database.

Syntax
```
SELECT column_name (s)
FROM table_name
```

SQL statements are not case sensitive. SELECT is the same as select.

To get PHP executes SQL statements with the mysql_query ( ) function. This function is used to send a query or command to a MySQL connection. The * character selects all of the data in the table. A script that selects all the data stored in the Person table is detailed in Figure E34.

```
<html>
<body>
<?php
// Connect to MySQL
$con = mysql_connect ("localhost", "joe", "tqr496");
if (!$con)
{
  die ('Could not connect: ' . mysql_error ( ));
} // End if
mysql_select_db ("my_db", $con);
// Create a recordset for the person table
$result = mysql_query ("SELECT * FROM person");
// Access the data in the result by record row order
```

```
while ($row = mysql_fetch_array ($result))
{
  echo $row [ 'FirstName' ] . " " . $row [ 'LastName' ];
  echo "<br />";
} // End while
mysql_close ($con);
?>
</body>
</html>
```
Figure E34. Select Data from a Database Table

The script in Figure E34 stores the data returned by the mysql_query ( ) function in the $result variable. Next, we use the mysql_fetch_array ( ) function to return the first row from the record set as an array. Each subsequent call to mysql_fetch_array ( ) returns the next row in the record set. The while loop loops through all the records in the record set to print the value of each row, we use the PHP $row variable ($row['FirstName'] and $row['LastName']).

The output of the code in Figure D34 will be:

James   Griffin
Glenn   Matthew

Figure E35 details the display of a select statement in a HTML table.

```
<html>
<body>
<?php
// Connect to MySQL
$con = mysql_connect ("localhost", "joe", "tqr496");
if (!$con)
{
  die ('Could not connect: ' . mysql_error ( ));
} // End if
// Select a database my_db
mysql_select_db ("my_db", $con);
// Create a recordset
$result = mysql_query ("SELECT * FROM person");
// Generate an open table tag
```

```
echo "<table border='1'>
// Setup a table header
<tr>
<th>Firstname</th>
<th>Lastname</th>
</tr>";
// Output the data in the recordset by record rows in a HTML table.
while ($row = mysql_fetch_array ($result))
{
  echo "<tr>";
  echo "<td>" . $row [ 'FirstName' ] . "</td>";
  echo "<td>" . $row [ 'LastName'  . "</td>";
  echo "</tr>";
} // End while
// Create an end of tagle HTML tag
echo "</table>";
// Close the MySQL connection
mysql_close ($con);
?>
</body>
<html>
```

Figure E35. Select Data from a Database Table and Display Information in a HTML Table

The output of the code in Figure E35 will be:

Firstname	Lastname
Glenn	Matthew
James	Griffin

E2.14. PHP MySQL The Where Clause

To select only data that matches a specified criterion, add a WHERE-clause to the SELECT-statement.

E2.14.1. The WHERE clause

To select only data that matches a specific criterion, add a WHERE-clause to the SELECT-statement.

Syntax
SELECT column FROM table
WHERE column operator value

The following operators can be used with the WHERE clause:

Operator	Description
=	Equal
!=	Not equal
>	Greater than
<	Less than
>=	Greater than or equal
<=	Less than or equal
BETWEEN	Between an inclusive range
LIKE	Search for a pattern

SQL statements are not case sensitive. WHERE is the same as where.

PHP executes SQL statement with the mysql_query ( ) function. This function is used to send a query or command to a MySQL connection.

Select all rows from the Person table, where FirstName='James' in Figure E36.

```php
<html>
<body>
<?php
// Connect to MySQL
$con = mysql_connect ("localhost", "joe", "tqr496");
if (!$con)
{
  die ('Could not connect: ' . mysql_error ( ));
} // End if
// Select a database my_db
mysql_select_db ("my_db", $con);
// Create a recordset
$result = mysql_query ("SELECT * FROM person
WHERE FirstName = 'James'");
// Display the information by rows
while ($row = mysql_fetch_array ($result))
```

```
{
  echo $row [ 'FirstName' ] . " " . $row [ 'LastName' ];
  echo "<br />";
} // End while
?>
</body>
</html>
```

Figure E36. Select Statement with Where Clause

The output of the code in Figure E36 will be:

James Griffin

E2.15. PHP MySQL Order by Keyword

The ORDER BY keyword is used to sort the data in a record set.

Syntax
```
SELECT column_name (s)
FROM table_name
ORDER BY column_name
```

SQL statements are not case sensitive. ORDER BY is the same as order by.

A query that selects all the data stored in the Person table, and sorts the result by the "Age" column:

```
<html>
<body>
<?php
// MySQL connection
$con = mysql_connect ("localhost", "joe", "tqr496");
if (!$con)
{
  die ('Could not connect: ' . mysql_error ( ));
} // End if
// Select database my_db
mysql_select_db ("my_db", $con);
// Create a recordset
```

```
$result = mysql_query ("SELECT * FROM person ORDER BY age");
// Display the recordset information by rows
while ($row = mysql_fetch_array ($result))
{
  echo $row [ 'FirstName' ]
  echo " " . $row [ 'LastName' ];
  echo " " . $row [ 'Age' ];
  echo "<br />";
} // End while
// Close the MySQL connection
mysql_close ($con);
?>
</body>
</html>
```
Figure E37. Order by Keyword

The output of the code in Figure E37 will be:

Glenn Matthew 33
James Griffin 35

E2.16. Sort Ascending or Descending

If you use the ORDER BY keyword, the sort-order of the record set is ascending by default (1 before 9 and "a" before "p").

Use the DESC keyword to specify a descending sort-order (9 before 1 and "p" before "a"):

```
SELECT column_name (s)
FROM table_name
ORDER BY column_name DESC
```

E2.16.1. Order by Two Columns

It is possible to order by more than one column. When ordering by more than one column, the second column is only used if the values in the first column are identical:

```
SELECT column_name (s)
```

FROM table_name
ORDER BY column_name1, column_name2

E2.16.2. PHP MySQL Update

The UPDATE statement is used to modify data in a database table.

Syntax
UPDATE table_name
SET column_name = new_value
WHERE column_name = some_value

Figure E38 updates some data in the Person table.

```
<html>
<body>
<?php
$con = mysql_connect ("localhost", "joe", "tqr496");
if (!$con)
{
  die ('Could not connect: ' . mysql_error ( ));
} // End if
mysql_select_db ("my_db", $con);
mysql_query ("UPDATE Person SET Age = '36'
WHERE FirstName = 'James' AND LastName = 'Griffin'");
mysql_close ($con);
?>
</body>
</html>
```
Figure E38. Update Statement

The Person table view after executing the script in Figure E38.

FirstName	LastName	Age
James	Griffin	36
Glenn	Matthew	33

E2.17. PHP MySQL Delete From

The DELETE FROM statement is used delete rows from a database table.

E2.18. Delete Data In a Database

The DELETE FROM statement is used to delete records from a database table.

Syntax
<DELETE FROM table_name
WHERE column_name = some_value

The script in Figure E39 deletes all the records in the Person table where LastName='Griffin'.

```
<html>
<body>
<?php
// Connect to MySQL
$con = mysql_connect("localhost", "joe", "tqr496");
if (!$con)
{
 die ('Could not connect: ' . mysql_error ( ));
}
// Select database my_db
mysql_select_db ("my_db", $con);
// Execute a delete from statement
mysql_query ("DELETE FROM Person WHERE LastName='Griffin'");
// Close the MySQL connection
mysql_close ($con);
?>
</body>
</html>
```
Figure E39. Delete From Statement

Figure E39 details a deletion statement from the person table.

FirstName	LastName	Age
Glenn	Matthew	33

E2.19. PHP Array Functions

The array functions allow you to manipulate arrays. PHP supports both simple and multi-dimensional arrays. There are also specific functions for populating arrays from database queries.

Function	Description	PHP
array ( )	Creates an array	3
array_change_key_case( )	Returns an array with all keys in lowercase or uppercase	4
array_chunk( )	Splits an array into chunks of arrays	4
array_combine( )	Creates an array by using one array for keys and another for its values	5
array_count_values( )	Returns an array with the number of occurrences for each value	4
array_diff( )	Compares array values, and returns the differences	4
array_diff_assoc( )	Compares array keys and values, and returns the differences	4
array_diff_key( )	Compares array keys, and returns the differences	5
array_diff_uassoc( )	Compares array keys and values, with an additional user-made function check, and returns the differences	5
array_diff_ukey( )	Compares array keys, with an additional user-made function check, and returns the differences	5
array_fill( )	Fills an array with values	4
array_filter( )	Filters elements of an array using a user-made function	4
array_flip( )	Exchanges all keys with their associated values in an array	4
array_intersect( )	Compares array values, and returns the matches	4
array_intersect_assoc( )	Compares array keys and values, and returns the matches	4
array_intersect_key( )	Compares array keys,	

	and returns the matches	5
array_intersect_uassoc( )	Compares array keys and values, with an additional user-made function check, and returns the matches	5
array_intersect_ukey( )	Compares array keys, with an additional user-made function check, and returns the matches	5
array_key_exists( )	Checks if the specified key exists in the array	4
array_keys( )	Returns all the keys of an array	4
array_map( )	Sends each value of an array to a user-made function, which returns new values	4
array_merge( )	Merges one or more arrays into one array	4
array_merge_recursive( )	Merges one or more arrays into one array	4
array_multisort( )	Sorts multiple or multi-dimensional arrays	4
array_pad( )	Inserts a specified number of items, with a specified value, to an array	4
array_pop( )	Deletes the last element of an array	4
array_product( )	Calculates the product of the values in an array	5
array_push( )	Inserts one or more elements to the end of an array	4
array_rand( )	Returns one or more random keys from an array	4
array_reduce( )	Returns an array as a string, using a user-defined function	4
array_reverse( )	Returns an array in the reverse order	4
array_search( )	Searches an array for a given value and returns the key	4
array_shift( )	Removes the first element from an array, and returns the value of the removed element	4
array_slice( )	Returns selected parts of an array	4
array_splice( )	Removes and replaces specified elements of an array	4
array_sum( )	Returns the sum of the values in an array	4
array_udiff( )	Compares array values in a user-made function and returns an array	5

array_udiff_assoc( )	Compares array keys, and compares array values in a user-made function, and returns an array	5
array_udiff_uassoc( )	Compares array keys and array values in user-made functions, and returns an array	5
array_uintersect( )	Compares array values in a user-made function and returns an array	5
array_uintersect_assoc( ) array values	Compares array keys, and compares in a user-made function, and returns an array	5
array_uintersect_uassoc( )	Compares array keys and array values in user-made functions, and returns an array	5
array_unique( )	Removes duplicate values from an array	4
array_unshift( )	Adds one or more elements to the beginning of an array	4
array_values( )	Returns all the values of an array	4
array_walk( )	Applies a user function to every member of an array	3
array_walk_recursive( )	Applies a user function recursively to every member of an array	5
arsort( )	Sorts an array in reverse order and maintain index association	3
asort( )	Sorts an array and maintain index association	3
compact( )	Create array containing variables and their values	4
count( )	Counts elements in an array, or properties in an object	3
current( )	Returns the current element in an array	3
each( )	Returns the current key and value pair from an array	3
end( )	Sets the internal pointer of an array to its last element	3
extract( )	Imports variables into the current symbol tablefrom an array	3
in_array( )	Checks if a specified value exists in an array	4
key( )	Fetches a key from an array	3
krsort( )	Sorts an array by key in reverse order	3

ksort( )	Sorts an array by key	3
list( )	Assigns variables as if they were an array	3
natcasesort( )	Sorts an array using a case insensitive "natural order" algorithm	4
natsort( )	Sorts an array using a "natural order" algorithm	4
next( )	Advance the internal array pointer of an array	3
pos( )	Alias of current( )	3
prev( )	Rewinds the internal array pointer	3
range( )	Creates an array containing a range of elements	3
reset( )	Sets the internal pointer of an array to its first element	3
rsort( )	Sorts an array in reverse order	3
shuffle( )	Shuffles an array	3
sizeof( )	Alias of count( )	3
sort( )	Sorts an array	3
uasort( )	Sorts an array with a user-defined function and maintain index association	3
uksort( )	Sorts an array by keys using a user-defined function	3
usort( )	Sorts an array by values using a user-defined function	3

E2.20. PHP Array Constants

PHP supports Array constants.

Constant	Description
CASE_LOWER	Used with array_change_key_case( ) to convert array keys to lower case
CASE_UPPER	Used with array_change_key_case( ) to convert array keys to upper case
SORT_ASC	Used with array_multisort( ) to sort in ascending order
SORT_DESC	Used with array_multisort( ) to sort in descending order

SORT_REGULAR   Used to compare items normally
SORT_NUMERIC   Used to compare items numerically
SORT_STRING   Used to compare items as strings
SORT_LOCALE_STRING   Used to compare items as strings,
                            based on the current locale   4

COUNT_NORMAL
COUNT_RECURSIVE
EXTR_OVERWRITE
EXTR_SKIP
EXTR_PREFIX_SAME
EXTR_PREFIX_ALL
EXTR_PREFIX_INVALID
EXTR_PREFIX_IF_EXISTS
EXTR_IF_EXISTS
EXTR_REFS

E2.21. PHP Calendar Functions

E2.21.1. PHP Calendar Introduction

The calendar functions are useful when working with different calendar formats. The standard it is based on is the Julian day count. Julian day count is a count of days starting from January 1, 4713 B.C.. The Julian day count is not the same as the Julian calendar.

To convert between calendar formats, first convert to Julian day count, then to the calendar format.

E2.21.2. PHP Calendar Functions

PHP supports the calendar functions.

Function	Description	PHP
cal_days_in_month( )	Returns the number of days in a month for a specified year and calendar	4
cal_from_jd( )	Converts a Julian day count into a date of a specified calendar	4
cal_info( )	Returns information about a given calendar	4
cal_to_jd( )	Converts a date to Julian day count	4

easter_date( )	Returns the Unix timestamp for midnight on Easter of a specified year	3
easter_days( )	Returns the number of days after March 21, on which Easter falls for a specified year	3
FrenchToJD( )	Converts a French Republican date to a Julian day count	3
GregorianToJD( )	Converts a Gregorian date to a Julian day count	3
JDDayOfWeek( )	Returns the day of a week	3
JDMonthName( )	Returns a month name	3
JDToFrench( )	Converts a Julian day count to a French Republican date	3
JDToGregorian( )	Converts a Julian day count to a Gregorian date	3
jdtojewish( )	Converts a Julian day count to a Jewish date	3
JDToJulian( )	Converts a Julian day count to a Julian date	3
jdtounix( )	Converts a Julian day count to a Unix timestamp	4
JewishToJD( )	Converts a Jewish date to a Julian day count	3
JulianToJD( )	Converts a Julian date to a Julian day count	3
unixtojd( )	Converts a Unix timestamp to a Julian day count	4

E2.21.3. PHP Calendar Constants

PHP supports the calendar constant.

Constant	Description	PHP
CAL_GREGORIAN	Gregorian calendar	3
CAL_JULIAN	Julian calendar	3
CAL_JEWISH	Jewish calendar	3
CAL_FRENCH	French Republican calendar	3
CAL_NUM_CALS		3

CAL_DOW_DAYNO		3
CAL_DOW_SHORT	3	
CAL_DOW_LONG	3	
CAL_MONTH_GREGORIAN_SHORT		3
CAL_MONTH_GREGORIAN_LONG		3
CAL_MONTH_JULIAN_SHORT		3
CAL_MONTH_JULIAN_LONG		3
CAL_MONTH_JEWISH	3	
CAL_MONTH_FRENCH	3	
CAL_EASTER_DEFAULT	4	
CAL_EASTER_DEFAULT	4	
CAL_EASTER_ROMAN	4	
CAL_EASTER_ALWAYS_GREGORIAN		4
CAL_EASTER_ALWAYS_JULIAN		4
CAL_JEWISH_ADD_ALAFIM_GERESH		5
CAL_JEWISH_ADD_ALAFIM		5
CAL_JEWISH_ADD_GERESHAYIM		5

E2.22. PHP HTTP

E2.22.1. PHP HTTP Introduction

The HTTP functions let you manipulate information sent to the browser by the Web server, before any other output has been sent.

E2.22.2. PHP HTTP Functions

PHP supports the HTTP function.

Function	Description	PHP
header( )	Sends a raw HTTP header to a client	3
headers_list( )	Returns a list of response headers sent (or ready to send)	5
headers_sent( )	Checks if / where the HTTP headers have been sent	3
setcookie( )	Sends an HTTP cookie to a client	3

setrawcookie( )   Sends an HTTP cookie without
                                   URL encoding the cookie value   5

Note: This is a modification of selected information from [11, 16].

Appendix F
Selected MySQL Tutorial

Databases are used to store and retrieve data from all sectors of our society. Most household and business enterprises have requirements to store vast amounts of data. A database that is implemented, interfaced, and accessed by client machines on a computer is often termed a database server. Database severs may be accessed by client computers on intranets and the World Wide Web Internet.

A standard language called Structured Query Language (SQL) allows many database applications to be shared on various computer platforms. One of the fastest relational database servers is called MySQL. MySQL implements a database parser for SQL. An array of options and capabilities are available for users to obtain various views of their data. MySQL is free for private and commercial use under licensing agreements. MySQL is available for download at http://www.mysql.com.

MySQL capabilities range across a number of topics, including the following:

- Ability to handle a large number of simultaneous users.
- Capacity to handle 50,000,000+ records.
- Very fast command execution.
- Easy and efficient user privilege system.

This database server has gained enormous popularity within the public and private sector. This tutorial will aid the reader in learning selected basic operations of the MySQL server, including how to make a proper connection, set up the server for consequential manipulation, and execute basic commands. The selected commands in this tutorial form the basis for the more advanced commands.

Many internet service providers (ISP) offer access to their MySQL database server. Some ISPs require the user to request MySQL before it can be used. After a request for MySQL service, a user account is established and configured.

187

F1. At First Glance

MySQL is most commonly entered through telnet. A nice Telnet program called Easyterm, can be found at http://www.arachnoid.com. Once the telnet connection to the web server has been accomplished, a second command provides access to the MySQL server. The procedure to make a connection and access to MySQL is:

1. Connect to telnet. This involves the insertion of the given ISP username and password.

mysql > login: user_id
mysql > Password: ********

2. Connect to MySQL. This involves the insertion of the username and password given specifically for MySQL use. This information is provided with your request to the ISP provider access MySQL.

mysql > mysql -u user_id -p

Syntax: mysql -h hostname -u username -p[password]
Or
mysql -h hostname -u username --password=password [database_name]

The user will then be prompted for a password, as prompted by -p.
Enter password: *******
Assuming MySQL has been correctly installed and configured, the user will see output similar to the following:

Welcome to the MySQL monitor. Commands end with ; or \g.
Your MySQL connection id is 4 to server version: 5.0.17-nt
Type 'help;' or "\h" for help. Type "\c" to clear the buffer.

mysql>

Users should resolve errors by consulting the MySQL documentation included with the software and instructions from your ISP provider. Once connected to the database, users are free to execute the various commands of the MySQL language. However before Users are able to select a database after they are connected to the MySQL server. The database selection command is use database name:

mysql> use user_id;
Result:
Database changed
mysql>

You now are connected to the database. Almost all commands in MySQL are followed by a semi-colon. A number of administrative commands can be viewed by typing help, \h or ? at the command line:

mysql> help

?	(\h)	Synonym for `help`.
clear	(\c)	Clear command.
connect	(\r)	Reconnect to the server. Optional arguments are db and host.
delimiter	(\d)	Set statement delimiter. NOTE: Take the rest of the line as new delimiter.
ego	(G)	Send command to mysql server, display results vertically.
exit	(\)	Exit mysql. Same as quit.
go	(\g)	Send command to mysql server.
help	(\h)	Display this help.
notee	(\t)	Don't write into outfile.
print	(\p)	print current command.
prompt	(\R)	Change your mysql prompt.
quit	(\q)	Quit mysql.
rehash	(\#)	Rebuild completion hash.
source	(\.)	Execute a mysql script file. Takes a file name as the argument.
status	(\s)	Get status information from the server
use	(\u)	Use another database. Takes database name as argument.
warnings	(\W)	Show warnings after every statement.

For sever side help, type 'help contents'
mysql>

These functions are immediately useful. Functions such as: status, use, prints, connect, clear, and quit will be very useful. These functions apply basic information to connect to the server, select the database, and perform basic commands. The next section will cover the concepts and techniques needed to properly setup the database for manipulation.

F2.0. Datatypes and Tables

A database is a collection of tables or relations, queries, reports, and other attributes that define a hierarchy of increasingly complex data structures. A table or relation is defined with unique column names. Each row of the table is a record or tuple of data. One column in the table has unique values and is called the primary key of the table.

These records are made up of the smallest object that can be manipulated by the user, known as the datatype. Together, one or more of these datatypes form a record. A table holds the collection of records that make up part of the database. We can consider the hierarchy of a database to be that of the following:

Database < Table < Record < Datatype

Datatypes come in several forms and sizes, allowing the programmer to create tables suited for the scope of a project. The decisions made in choosing proper datatypes greatly influence the performance of a database.

F2.1. MySQL Datatypes

MySQL is capable of many of the datatypes that programmer encounter in other programming languages. Some of the more commonly used MySQL datatypes include:

CHAR (M)
CHAR's are used to represent fixed length strings. A CHAR string can range from 1-255 characters. A CHAR stores the whole length of the declared variable, regardless of the size of the data contained within. Define a variable Toy and allocate it as a set of characters of length 15.
Toy CHAR (15);

VARCHAR (M)
VARCHAR is a more flexible form of the CHAR data type. It also represents data of type String and the data are in variable length format. Again, VARCHAR can hold 1-255 characters. VARCHAR can save database space, due to its variable length format characteristic. Define a variable Toy and allocate it as a string with a maximum length of 15.
Toy VARCHAR (15);

INT (M) [Unsigned]
The INT datatype stores integers ranging from -2147483648 to 2147483647. An optional "unsigned" integer can be denoted with the declaration, modifying the range to be 0 to 4294967295. Example of valid and invalid integers defined for the variable myint is:
myint INT;
Valid integer: '-24567'.   Invalid integer: '3000000000'.
myint INT unsigned;
Valid integer: '3000000000'.   Invalid integer: '-24567'.

FLOAT [(M, D)]
A FLOAT represents small decimal numbers, used when a precise representation of a number is required. Define a floating point variable temperature with 4 digits of which two digits are decimal fractions.
temperature FLOAT (4, 2);

This could be used to represent temperature, which could be a decimal value. Several valid and invalid temperatures are:
42.35 is valid, accurately represented.
324.45 is invalid, rounded to 324.5.
2.2 is valid, accurately represented.
34.542 is invalid, rounded to 34.54.
FLOAT is rounded. Use DECIMAL as a datatype for money. The DECIMAL datatype is detailed in the MySQL documentation.

DATE
Stores date related information. The default format is 'YYYY-MM-DD', and ranges from '0000-00-00' to '9999-12-31'. Review the MySQL documentation for a complete set of date formatting and manipulation commands. Define a variable mydate as:
mydate DATE;

TEXT / BLOB
The text and blob datatypes are used when a string of 255 - 65535 characters is required to be stored. This is useful when one would need to store document such as the Selected MySQL Tutorial. The only difference between BLOB and TEXT is that TEXT is compared case insensitively, while BLOB is compared case sensitively.

SET
A datatype of type string that allows one to choose from a designated set of values, one value or several values. One can designate up to 64 values. Define a variable tool as SET.
tool SET ("socket", "wedge") NOT NULL;
The following values can be held by tool:
""

"socket"
"wedge"
"socket,wedge"

ENUM
A datatype of type string that has the same characteristics as the SET datatype, but only one set of allowed values may be chosen. Usually this only takes up one byte of space, thus saving time and space within a table. Define a variable pool as EMUN.
pool ENUM ("socket", "wedge") NOT NULL;
The following values can be held by pool:
" "

"socket"
"wedge"

Records
A group of declared datatypes form a record. A record is one data variable or as many data variables. One or more records form the structure of a table.

F2.2. The Bigger Picture: Tables

Before we can execute commands on the database, we must first create a table in which data can be stored. This is accomplished in the following MySQL command:
mysql> CREATE TABLE first (
> name VARCHAR (15),
> email VARCHAR (25),
> phone_number INT,
> ID INT NOT NULL AUTO_INCREMENT,
> PRIMARY KEY (ID));
Ensuing output:
Query OK, 0 rows affected (0.10 sec)
mysql>

The first table in your database has now been created. No two tables can have the same name and each dataspace is a unique column name.

F2.3. Column Name Characteristics:

A name may not be made up of strictly numbers.
A name may start with a number.
A name may be up to 64 characters.
A name may include under-score to connect compound components.

Other table options:
The following options can be placed after any datatype, adding other characteristics and capabilities to them.
Primary Key. Used to differentiate one record from another. No two records can have the same primary key.
Auto_Increment. A column with this function is automatically incremented one value (previous + 1) when an insertion is made into the record. The datatype is automatically incremented when 'NULL' is inserted into the column.
NOT NULL. Signifies that the column can never be assigned a NULL value.

An example of a primary key definition for a column name soc_sec_number is:
soc_sec_number INT PRIMARY KEY;   No two soc_sec_number records can hold the same value.

Define a primary key for a column name ID_NUMBER with AUTO_INCREMENT.
ID_NUMBER INT AUTO_INCREMENT;
Automatically increments in value, starting at '1', with every subsequent insertion.

F2.4. Table-Relevant Commands

We can execute a number of useful commands pertaining to the tables, such as the following:

Show Tables
mysql> show tables;
Result:
This will list all tables currently existing within the database.

Show Columns
mysql> show columns from test;
Result:
This will return the columns and column information pertaining to the designated table.

Describe Table
mysql> describe table_name;
Results:
This returns the columns and datatypes for the table. table_name is the name of an existing table in the database.

Alter Table
mysql> alter table_name;
Results:
This allows the user to modify the structure of the table. table_name is the name of an existing table in the database.

Execute show tables, show columns from, and describe commands after you have created the test table called first. These commands will be helpful as your database increases in size and complexity. Creation of tables is one of the most important concepts of the MySQL server. Tables are constructed using datatypes, which when grouped together form a record. Good table designs reduce application complex cities and aids in manipulation of data in tables in the database.

F3. Manipulating the Database

A database can be manipulated in four possible ways: addition, deletion, modification, and search. These topics briefly covered in Sections F3.1 through F3.4. Database manipulations are accomplished with a Structured Query Language (SQL). The Structured Query Language is defined with a structure or syntax for each command. A command interpreter or database engine implements SQL in the database system. The slightest error in placement of a parentheses, comma, or semicolon will almost surely end in error. As a result, take care to be attentive of command syntax.

F3.1. Insertion of Records

The originally created table, first, created in the section F2.0. **Datatypes and Tables** under F2.2. The Bigger Picture: Tables will be used as the examples in this section. The table first is defined again as:

```
mysql> CREATE TABLE first (
> name VARCHAR (15),
> email VARCHAR (25),
> phone_number INT,
> ID INT NOT NULL AUTO_INCREMENT,
> PRIMARY KEY (ID));
```

Insertion of data into the table is accomplished, logically enough, using the INSERT command.
```
mysql> INSERT INTO first VALUES
mysql> ('Henry Jones', 'carrots@atm.com',
mysql> 5554321, NULL);
```
Result, assuming the command was correctly entered:
Query OK, 1 row affected (0.02 sec)
mysql>

Coding actions review for the INSERT INTO command:
Single quotations were placed around the datatypes VARCHAR. All datatypes of type STRING (i.e. char, varchar, text, blob, etc.) must be surrounded in single quotes, or an error will occur.
There were no single quotes surrounding the phone number. Datatypes of type INT do not require single quotes.
NULL? A NULL allows any datatype with the characteristic AUTO_INCREMENT to be automatically assigned a value. If it is the first record inserted into the database, it is assigned the value '1'. Otherwise, it is assigned the previously inserted value + 1 (i.e. if the previously inserted value was '2', then the next would be '3'). In addition, the insertion of NULL into a variable of type TIMESTAMP causes that variable to be given the value of the current date.

It is of importance to remember that the same number of values must be inserted as datatypes are contained within a record. In the insertion example in this section, if one attempted to insert only three values instead of four, the insertion would fail. The same result applies if one attempted to insert five values.

An error insert into first command is:
```
mysql> insert into first values('doggy');
ERROR 1058: Column count doesn't match value count
mysql>
```

One of the advantageous aspects of MySQL is its ability to convert without trouble between datatypes. MySQL automatically converts between integers, strings, and dates.

F3.2. Selection

The select statement allows the user to search and extract data from tables in the database.

```
mysql> SELECT * FROM first
mysql> WHERE (name = "Henry Jones");
```

Result:

name	email	phone	ID
Henry Jones	carrots@atm.com	5554321	1

Let's assume we have inserted four differing records, all bearing the same name of "Henry Jones", yet having different email addresses and phone numbers. The table first, would look somewhat like Figure :

name	email	phone	ID
Henry Jones	carrots@atm.com	5554321	1
Henry Jones	peppers@atm.com	5554331	2
Henry Jones	lettuce@atm.com	5554341	3
Henry Jones	celery@atm.com	5554351	4

Figure F1. Select Command Output

F3.3. Deletion

One can also delete records inserted into the table. This is accomplished through the DELETE command.

```
mysql> DELETE FROM first
mysql>  WHERE (name = "Henry Jones");
```

Result:

This would result in the deletion of all records within the table first containing name "Bugs Bunny".

Another example:
mysql> DELETE FROM first
mysql> WHERE (phone_number = 5554321);

Result: (Using the state of the first table in Figure F1)

name	email	phone	ID
Henry Jones	peppers@atm.com	5554331	2
Henry Jones	lettuce@atm.com	5554341	3
Henry Jones	celery@atm.com	5554351	4

F3.4. Modification

MySQL also has the capability of modifying data already entered into the table. This is accomplished through the UPDATE command.
mysql> UPDATE first SET name = 'Jerry Smith'
mysql> WHERE name = "Henry Jones";

name	email	phone	ID
Jerry Smith	peppers@devshed.com	5554331	2
Jerry Smith	lettuce@devshed.com	5554341	3
Jerry Smith	celery@devshed.com	5554351	4

This section, we covered the core MySQL database manipulation functions, basic insertion, deletion, modification, and search. The next Section F4.0 will elaborate on these capabilities, providing extended functioning and flexibility when manipulating the database.

F4. 0. Advanced MySQL Commands

We have covered selected commands that describe a small part of MySQL capabilities. A few advanced MySQL commands are explored to apply MySQL commands and to encourage users to search the web for other MySQL documentation.

F4.1. Logical Operations

MySQL includes full support of all basic logical operations.

AND (&&)
mysql> SELECT * FROM first WHERE
mysql> (name = "Henry Jones") AND
mysql> (phone_number = 5554321);
Result:
All records containing the name "Henry Jones" AND the phone number '5554321' will be displayed to the screen.

OR (||)
mysql> SELECT * FROM first WHERE
mysql> (name = "Henry Jones") OR
mysql> (phone_number = 5554321);
Result:
All records containing the name "Henry Jones" OR the phone number '5554321' will be displayed to the screen.

NOT (!)
mysql> SELECT * FROM first WHERE
mysql> (name != "Henry Jones");
Result:
All records NOT containing the name "Henry Jones" will be displayed to the screen.

Order By
mysql> SELECT * FROM first WHERE
mysql> (name = "Henry Jones") ORDER BY
mysql> phone_number;
Result:
All records containing the name "Bugs Bunny" will be displayed to the screen, ordered in respect to the phone number.

F4.2. Search Functions

MySQL offers the user the ability to perform both general and specific searches on data.
mysql> SELECT * FROM first WHERE
mysql> (name LIKE "%ry Jones ");
Result:

All records containing the partial string "ry Jones" will be displayed to the screen. This would include such names as: "Henry Jones", "nry Jones", "ry Jones", and "234rtry Jones".

Notice that "LIKE" has been used instead of the equals sign (=). "LIKE" signifies that one is searching for an estimate of the data requested, and not necessarily an exact copy.

F4.3. Focused Search Results

One can also perform searches and display only certain columns.
mysql> SELECT name FROM first WHERE
mysql> (name = "Henry Jones");
Result:

name
Henry Jones

F4.4. Alter table

Another very important function of MySQL is the ability to modify previously created tables. This is accomplished via the ALTER statement. This function allows one to add, modify, and delete columns, as well as rename the table, among other functions.

Example: Rename the table
mysql> ALTER table first RENAME mytest;

Example: Add a column
mysql> ALTER table mytest ADD birthday DATE;

Example: Modify a column
mysql> ALTER table mytest CHANGE
mysql> name newname VARCHAR (25);
Example: Delete a column
mysql> ALTER table mytest DROP newname;

Executing the four functions in the examples would modify first, creating the following table:
mysql> TABLE mytest (
> email VARCHAR (25),
> phone_number INT,

```
> ID INT AUTO_INCREMENT,
> birthday DATE);
```

The topics covered within this tutorial are but a short introduction of the capabilities of MySQL. However, these functions form the basis of almost all advanced commands to be found in the language. Remember is to practice and study the documentation to enhance your skills in MySQL. This is a modification of selected information from [14, 17].

Appendix G
Selected Networking Tutorial

G1. Apache Installation

Many Linux and Unix operating systems include Apache. In this case, follow the operating systems documentation to start and configure the Apache server software.

The installation of the UNIX and Linux version of Apache is just like installing most other applications under these operating systems. Download the source, compile it, or the executable image and install the executable code. Windows is easy for users to install Apache. Apache is installed in Windows with a setup wizard.

Depending on the platform Apache range from 1 to 3 megabytes (MB) in size. After downloading Apache it is just a matter of installing it.

G1.2. Download Apache

Connect to the World Wide Web and access the Apache website at http://www.apache.org/. Select downloads option and get a copy of Apache.

G1.2.1. UNIX or Linux Operating System

Review the named files list and select a UNIX or Linux version of Apache. Grab the gzipped copy of Apache. The Apache file name is apache_version.extension. Version is of the form digit.digit.digit, where digit = 1 | 2 | 3 | 4 | 5 | 6 | 7 | 8 | 9. Extension is tar for UNIX and Linux. Windows operating system extension is exe.

Decompress the tar ball file. Simply type
tar -zxf apache_version.tar.gz

A directory called apache_version will be created. Change to this directory to compile the source code.

G1.2.1.1. Compiling the Source

With all the source code placed in the decompressed tar ball directory and sub-directories, compile Apache to make it work. Use GNU cc or the gcc compiler to compile the source. The gcc compiler is free and distributed with most UNIX and Linux operating systems. If it is not on your computer, download and install it from http://www.fsf.org/software/gcc/gcc.html.

In the apache_version directory, from the prompt type
./configure

This will create a makefile with the default configuration. To change the configuration, you must edit apache_version/src/Configuration.tmpl before running configure. You can add/remove modules from the list, and many other options. Normally the defaults are used in the server application. For more information on editing the Configuration file, check out the README.configure file included with the distribution.

Command line commands to type are:

make

to compile the server, and

make install

to put it in the proper directories. The default is /usr/local/apache/, though this can be changed in Configuration.tmpl.

Apache binaries are finally installed.

G1.2.2. Windows Operating System

Download the Windows version binary setup file.

Double click the downloaded file and the setup wizard will open and install the server.

During the installation, you will be asked for
the directory to install Apache into
the start menu name
the installation type. Typical installs everything except the source code. Minimum doesn't install the manuals or source code, and Custom allows you to 'customize' what is installed.

G1.3. Using Apache

There are two methods for running Apache, one is for Windows and the other is for UNIX or Linux.

G1.3.1. Windows

Since Apache is just another Windows application, just go to the start menu, then the Apache Web Server program group. If you are not running Windows NT, just select "Start Apache as console app". If you are running Apache on NT though, you can hit the "Install Apache as Service (NT only)" option and Apache will be installed as a service on your computer. This means it will automatically start every time NT is booted up.
To shutdown the server, there are two other options available in the start menu that should be self-explanatory.

G1.3.2. UNIX or Linux

To startup Apache in UNIX or Linux, all you have to do is run httpd.

/usr/local/apache/httpd

This depends on where you installed the binary. It will automatically use the configuration file it created on compilation called httpd.conf. If you would like to use another configuration file, you can use the -f argument.

Example:
/usr/local/apache/httpd -f /usr/local/apache/conf/httpd.conf

The Apache distribution does come with another method of starting/stopping/ restarting Apache. The script is called apachectl. In the Apache src directory (apache_ version/src), type make at the prompt. You will see a few more files compiled. After make is done, go to the support directory (apache_version/src/support), where a bunch of new files are created. There are a few helper scripts made now, including apachectl, htpasswd that are used to make Apache passwords for protected directories. Make a copy of these two files to your Apache binary directory. The default setting for this directory is located at /usr/local/apache/bin/.

To start the server, use
/usr/local/apache/bin/apachectl start

There is also
/usr/local/apache/bin/apachectl stop

and
/usr/local/apache/bin/apachectl restart
available, obviously to stop or restart the server.

To have Apache start upon booting up your system, make a copy of apachectl in your startup directory, typically /etc/rc.d/init.d or /etc/rc3.d/....

Check it all out to make sure everything is working. From your browser, check out http://localhost/ right afterwards.

G1.4. Configuring Apache

The Apache configuration is found in the apache_version/conf/ directory. Three files httpd.conf, srm.conf, and access.conf are involved in the configuration.

The file httpd.conf contains directives and configurations relating to the operation of the server as a whole. Server logs and server management are controlled from this file.

A srm.conf file contains the configurations for the management of resources in the filesystem, such as aliases and directory indexes.

An access.conf file contains information on access control in choice directories.

Backup the Apache configuration in UNIX or Linux with a command similar to
cp httpd.conf-dist httpd.conf

Backup the Apache configuration in Windows by making a copy of the file and rename it.

Make the current configuration current. Restart Apache to start with any changes to the configuration files to take effect.

Appendix H
Implemented Client/Server Application

H1. Database Dump

```
-- MySQL dump 10.10
--
-- Host: localhost    Database: pdcrs
-- --------------------------------------------------------
-- Server version 5.0.17-nt

/*!40101 SET @OLD_CHARACTER_SET_CLIENT=@@CHARACTER_SET_
CLIENT */;
/*!40101 SET @OLD_CHARACTER_SET_RESULTS=@@CHARACTER_
SET_RESULTS */;
/*!40101 SET @OLD_COLLATION_CONNECTION=@@COLLATION_
CONNECTION */;
/*!40101 SET NAMES utf8 */;
/*!40103 SET @OLD_TIME_ZONE=@@TIME_ZONE */;
/*!40103 SET TIME_ZONE='+00:00' */;
/*!40014 SET @OLD_UNIQUE_CHECKS=@@UNIQUE_CHECKS,
UNIQUE_CHECKS=0 */;
/*!40014 SET @OLD_FOREIGN_KEY_CHECKS=@@FOREIGN_KEY_
CHECKS, FOREIGN_KEY_CHECKS=0 */;
/*!40101 SET @OLD_SQL_MODE=@@SQL_MODE, SQL_MODE='NO_
AUTO_VALUE_ON_ZERO' */;
/*!40111 SET @OLD_SQL_NOTES=@@SQL_NOTES, SQL_NOTES=0 */;

--
```

-- Current Database: `pdcrs`
--

CREATE DATABASE /*!32312 IF NOT EXISTS*/ `pdcrs` /*!40100 DEFAULT CHARACTER SET latin1 */;

USE `pdcrs`;
--
-- Table structure for table `pdata`
--

DROP TABLE IF EXISTS `pdata`;
CREATE TABLE `pdata` (
 `ID` mediumint(9) NOT NULL auto_increment,
 `orgname` varchar(35) default NULL,
 `bestpra` varchar(254) default NULL,
 `numprod` decimal(6,0) default NULL,
 `prodsale` decimal(10,2) default NULL,
 `numemp` decimal(6,0) default NULL,
 `modayr` date default NULL,
 PRIMARY KEY (`ID`)
) ENGINE=InnoDB DEFAULT CHARSET=latin1;

--
-- Dumping data for table `pdata`
--

/*!40000 ALTER TABLE `pdata` DISABLE KEYS */;
LOCK TABLES `pdata` WRITE;
INSERT INTO `pdata` VALUES (1,'Major Car ','This is a test of the performance system. ','50','45.98','23','2006-12-31'),(2,'Tall Tree Forest','The best ideas are all good and require research to complete the average project. ','56','125.00','85','2005-12-30');
UNLOCK TABLES;
/*!40000 ALTER TABLE `pdata` ENABLE KEYS */;

--
-- Table structure for table `profile`

```
--

DROP TABLE IF EXISTS `profile`;
CREATE TABLE `profile` (
 `ID` mediumint(9) NOT NULL auto_increment,
 `fname` varchar(30) default NULL,
 `lname` varchar(30) default NULL,
 `address` varchar(35) default NULL,
 `city` varchar(35) default NULL,
 `state` varchar(2) default NULL,
 `zipcode` varchar(10) default NULL,
 `phone` varchar(10) default NULL,
 `email` varchar(60) default NULL,
 PRIMARY KEY (`ID`)
) ENGINE=InnoDB DEFAULT CHARSET=latin1;


--

-- Dumping data for table `profile`

--



/*!40000 ALTER TABLE `profile` DISABLE KEYS */;
LOCK TABLES `profile` WRITE;
INSERT INTO `profile` VALUES (1,'John','Miller','3 T Street','James City','VA
','23687','3458769876','millerj@amt.com'),(2,'John','Henry','12 Manville Ave.','
Washington','DC','23430','932349452 ','westj@save.com ');
UNLOCK TABLES;
/*!40000 ALTER TABLE `profile` ENABLE KEYS */;


--

-- Table structure for table `users`

--


DROP TABLE IF EXISTS `users`;
CREATE TABLE `users` (
 `ID` mediumint(9) NOT NULL auto_increment,
 `username` varchar(60) default NULL,
 `password` varchar(60) default NULL,
 PRIMARY KEY (`ID`)
```

```
) ENGINE=InnoDB DEFAULT CHARSET=latin1;

--
-- Dumping data for table `users`
--

/*!40000 ALTER TABLE `users` DISABLE KEYS */;
LOCK TABLES `users` WRITE;
INSERT INTO `users` VALUES (1,'body','841a2d689ad86bd1611447453c22c6f
c'),(2,'book','821f03288846297c2cf43c34766a38f7');
UNLOCK TABLES;
/*!40000 ALTER TABLE `users` ENABLE KEYS */;
/*!40103 SET TIME_ZONE=@OLD_TIME_ZONE */;

/*!40101 SET SQL_MODE=@OLD_SQL_MODE */;
/*!40014 SET FOREIGN_KEY_CHECKS=@OLD_FOREIGN_KEY_CHECKS
*/;
/*!40014 SET UNIQUE_CHECKS=@OLD_UNIQUE_CHECKS */;
/*!40101 SET CHARACTER_SET_CLIENT=@OLD_CHARACTER_SET_
CLIENT */;
/*!40101 SET CHARACTER_SET_RESULTS=@OLD_CHARACTER_SET_
RESULTS */;
/*!40101 SET COLLATION_CONNECTION=@OLD_COLLATION_
CONNECTION */;
/*!40111 SET SQL_NOTES=@OLD_SQL_NOTES */;
```

About the Author

Dr. Edward Hill, Jr. has been in the information profession since 1964. He has held technical and managerial positions in government including: Mathematician, Computer Systems Analyst, Survey Statistician, and Supervisory Survey Statistician from 1964 -1996. He has worked as an Adjunct Associate Professor of Computer Science from 1978 - 1996 at Howard University. He has worked as an Associate Professor of Computer Science from 1996 - 2006 at Hampton University. He has been a Computer Science Consultant since 2000. Dr. Hill is a widely recognized expert in database design, computer information science, data resource management, and data-related planning, analysis, and design methods. He has taught many undergraduate and graduate courses in information management. Dr. Hill is distinguished by his ability to communicate concepts clearly, simply, and effectively to any audience detailing his experiences in computer science and other areas.

Dr. Hill is a graduate of Southern University (B.S. degree with major in mathematics/ education), Atlanta University (M.S. degree with major in mathematics), and The George Washington University at Washington, DC (D.Sc. with major in Computer Science, minors in Applied Mathematics and Operations Research)

Email: **ehill96@yahoo.com**

Index

978-0-595-45028-2
0-595-45028-8